Praise for *Putting Hope to Work*

"While some people may thrive in frenetic environments where the focus is limited to the basic delivery of results, many of us feel an emerging need for personal peace in the midst of organizational chaos. Hutson and Perry articulate clearly and succinctly the message of hope. Their five principles (possibility, agency, worth, openness, and connection) not only frame how to gain hope, but show that it can deliver enormous value to people, teams, and organizations. This is a book worth savoring. It offers a glimpse of what can and what should be in an ideal organization."

Dave Ulrich
Professor, Ross School of Business, University of Michigan
Partner, The RBL Group

"This is a wonderful exploration into the power of hope and what applying hope can do for an organization. In today's tumultuous business climate, where constant change is over-abundant, many organizations lose their way and morale suffers greatly. Something as simple and yet as complex as hope can mobilize a team and take them to a new level. This book is inspiring and refreshing, as no one has examined just how powerful and effective hope can be. I plan to take some of the stories and ideas shared in this book and put them into action immediately."

Deanna L. Leonard
VP of Design/Marketing/Merchandising, Sara Lee

"This book is a thoughtful and provocative reminder that when genuine (and realistic) hope is present in organizations, people think and act differently. In today's rapidly intensifying workplace, leaders need to balance their endless pursuit of efficiency with a healthy dose of inspiration and engagement. Even for those skeptics who don't believe 'hope makes all things possible,' this book will inspire you to more consciously create and nurture hope—for yourself but especially for others."

Scott Hughes
Senior Director, Global Consumer and Market Intelligence, The Wm. Wrigley Jr. Company

Putting Hope to Work

Five Principles to Activate Your Organization's Most Powerful Resource

HARRY HUTSON AND BARBARA PERRY

PRAEGER

Westport, Connecticut
London

Library of Congress Cataloging-in-Publication Data

Hutson, Harry.
  Putting hope to work : five principles to activate your organization's most powerful resource / Harry Hutson and Barbara Perry.
    p. cm.
  Includes bibliographical references and index.
  ISBN 0–275–98819–8 (alk. paper)
  1. Employee motivation. 2. Hope. 3. Leadership—Psychological aspects. 4. Organizational effectiveness—Psychological aspects. I. Perry, Barbara, 1943– II. Title.
HF5549.5.M63H88   2006
658.4′092–dc22   2006008235

British Library Cataloguing in Publication Data is available.

Library of Congress Catalog Card Number: 2006008235
ISBN: 0–275–98819–8

First published in 2006

Praeger Publishers, 88 Post Road West, Westport, CT 06881
An imprint of Greenwood Publishing Group, Inc.
www.praeger.com

Printed in the United States of America

The paper used in this book complies with the Permanent Paper Standard issued by the National Information Standards Organization (Z39.48-1984).

10 9 8 7 6 5 4 3 2 1

Harry: To my parents, Betty and Harry, whose hope for their family and friends is exceeded only by the love we return.

Barbara: To my children—Betsy, Flicka, Tod, and Autumn—you have taught me all I ever need to know about hope.

Contents

Acknowledgments

Heartfelt thanks to all of you who have helped us in some way, large or small, whether you know it or not. Apologies to any we have overlooked. The essence of this project has been to give voice to others, and to make sense of what we've heard. Our hope to have done this adequately well comes with full ownership of the gaps in our understanding and reportage.

Vicki Abrahmson, Michael Allen, Brad Anderson, Andy Arken, Breck Arnzen, Sheryl Ash, Becky Bacon, Bruce Bacon, Annie Barron, Liz Bergeron, Eli Berniker, Maggie Bidlingmaier, Patricia Blochowiak, John Boisvert, Minx Boren, Richard Boyatzis, Maddy Bragar, Judy Brain, Patricia Bruininks, Margaret Buchanan, Shirley Bunger, Lynn Cannici, Antonio Cano, Jennifer Cassettari, Barbara Cavalier, Son-Mey Chiu, Hayden Claisse, Marni Clippinger, Greg Collins, Michael Conforti, Nick Craig, Steve Dashe, Sandy Davis, Manpreet Dhillon, Diane Dixon, Christopher Drew, Barry Dym, Sally Edwards, Zac Edwards, Lou English, Peter Erickson, Marsha Everton, Ron Feinstein, Randy Ferguson, Lesley Ficarri, Al Fitz, Rick Ford, Sheree Ford, Kathy Foster, Amy Fradon, John Hope Franklin, Barbara Fredrickson, Gerry Gauthier, Roger Gerard, Randy Gier, Ellen Glanz, Ron Gleason, Linda Goodspeed, Renee Goodspeed, Joe Gottschalk, Beth Graham, Lydia Faxon Green, Ray Green, Annie Hagert, Cliff Hakim, Ned Hamson, Rob Hartz, Melissa Harwood, John Haskell, Geoff Hibner, Gay Hoagland, David Hohn, Karen Holseth-Brokema, Harry Hutson, Sr., Sally Hutson, Barbara Huzil, Kathleen Jamieson, Karen Janus, Fr. Gregory Jensen, Mike Kallenberger, Dacher Keltner, Pak Ken, Linda Klabacha, Scott Knous, Brian Knutson, JoAnne Koester, Theresa Korbos, Nancy Kosciolek, Eric Kramer, Laura Kubzansky, Carey Kyler, Bob Landis, Tom Lane, Ellen

Langer, Denise Larsen, Maxine Lauer, Sabra Lee, Lenora LeMay, Fred Loya, Jo Luck, Liane Luke, David Lykken, Sonja Lyubomirsky, David Malone, Geoff Martin, Teri McCaslin, Jay McLean, Steve Mynott, Chantha Nguon, Omar Noorzay, Rodney North, Ginny O'Brien, Frank Okrasinski, Dan O'Neill, Sarah Osmer, Cathy Pagliaro, Marsha Palitz-Eliott, Bill Pasmore, Lou Patterson, Christopher Peterson, Lani Peterson, Fred Pinciaro, Price Pritchett, Bob Rehm, Ric Reichard, Frank Rexach, Lisa Reynolds, Sylvia Reynolds, Susanne Rheault, Sally Ride, Margaret Rose, Zeda Rosenberg, Frank Rudolph, Charles Salyer, Dean Scarborough, Diane Scheurell, Kathi Seifert, Martin E.P. Seligman, Hal Shorey, Deb Slobodnik, Alan Slobodnik, Robert Smyth, C.R. Snyder, Michael Sonduck, Susaan Straus, Stephanie Streeter, Anne Suh, Keith Swayne, Earl Taylor, Ray Thorn, Todd Tillemans, Silvana Torik, George De La Torre, John Toussaint, Jim Votruba, Robyn Waters, Kittie Watson, Kaethe Weingarten, Marvin Weisbord, Craig Wildrick, Castle Wilson, Wendy Wilson-Bett, Ingrid Joy Wolfson, Nuala Woodham, Tom Wright, John Wurzburger, Susan Yashinsky, Thomas Yeomans, Jaime Yordan, Jay Zimmerman, and Eve Porter Zuckerman.

We also want to thank the librarians and staff at four Duke University libraries (Perkins Library, Divinity School Library, Medical School Library, and the Lilly Library), and the Davis Library at the University of North Carolina, Chapel Hill.

Our graphic artist, Summer Elton, contributed both concepts and visuals, and we are very grateful.

Finally, we are indebted to our agent, Rob McQuilken, and our editor, Nick Philipson, who were hopeful from the beginning.

The following sources are acknowledged for permissions to reproduce quotations that have been used as sidebars in the book.

Yehuda Amichai, *The Selected Poetry of Yehuda Amichai, Newly Revised and Expanded Edition*. Copyright © 1996 by Yehuda Amichai. Reprinted with permission of The University of California Press.

Ronald Aronson, "Hope After Hope?" *Social Research*, LVI, No. 2 (Summer, 1999), p. 491.

Attributed to Coleman Barks, retold by Elisa Davy Pearmain, ed., *Doorways to the Soul: 52 Wisdom Tales from Around the World* (Cleveland, OH: The Pilgrim Press, 1998), p. 51.

Kalliope Rodman Dalto, age 9, Barbara's granddaughter.

High Eagle, quoted in Lois S. Kelley, "Hope as Lived by Native Americans," Rosemarie Rizzo Parse, *Hope: An International Human Becoming Perspective* (Sudbury, MA: Jones and Bartlett Publishers, 1999), p. 261.

Alice Rose George and Lee Marks, "Introduction," *Hope Photographs*, ed. Alice Rose George and Lee Marks (London: Thames and Hudson, 1998), p. 9.

Vaclav Havel, *Disturbing the Peace: A Conversation with Karel Hvizdala* (New York: Alfred A. Knopf, 1990), p. 181.

Excerpt from Seamus Heaney, *The Cure at Troy: A Version of Sophocles's Philoctetes* (New York: The Noonday Press, 1991). Copyright © 1990 by Seamus Heaney. Reprinted by permission of Farrar, Straus and Giroux, LLC.

Ronna Fay Jevne, "Hope: The Simplicity and the Complexity," *Interdisciplinary Perspectives on Hope*, ed. Jaklin Eliott (New York: Nova Science Publishers, 2005), p. 268.

Barbara Kingsolver, *Animal Dreams* (New York, NY: HarperCollins, 1990), p. 299.

Andre Lacocque and Pierre-Emmanuel Lacocque, *The Jonah Complex* (Atlanta: John Knox Press, 1981), p. 54.

Maurice Lamm, *The Power of Hope: The One Essential of Life and Love* (New York: Simon & Schuster, 1997), p. 32.

Anne Lamott, "Scattering the Present," August 1, 2003, internet column.

John G. Neihardt, *Black Elk Speaks: Being the Life Story of a Holy Man of the Ogallala Sioux* (Lincoln: University of Nebraska Press, 1979), p. 43.

Mary Oliver, *Winter Hours: Prose, Prose Poems, and Poems* (Boston, MA: A Mariner Book, Houghton Mifflin, 2000), p. 93.

Elaine Pope and Larry Charles, "The Fix Up," Seinfeld episode no. 33, broadcast February 5, 1992.

Wallace Stevens, "*Notes Towards a Supreme Fiction*," in *Wallace Stevens: Collected Poetry and Prose*, ed. Frank Kermode and Joan Richardson (New York: Library of America, 1997), pp. 329 ff.

Introduction

Competence is essential, but it's not enough. The great voices of history have always been the voices of optimism and hope.[1]

Bob Herbert

We began more than ten years ago with the small idea that "driving out fear" was not the full solution to workplace malaise. At a Total Quality conference in the early 1990s, we attended a session called "Driving out Fear" based on one of the famous fourteen points of W. Edwards Deming, "Drive out fear so that everyone may work more effectively for the company." In *Out of the Crisis*, Deming described actual expressions of fear in the workplace, fear that defeats knowledge and impairs performance:

"I am afraid that I may lose my job because my company will go out of business...."

"I could do my job better if I understood what happens next."

"I am afraid to put forth an idea. I'd be guilty of treason if I did...."

"I am afraid that I may not always have an answer when my boss asks something...."

"I am afraid to admit a mistake."

"My boss believes in fear...."

"The system that I work in will not permit me to expand my ability...."[2]

We had attended a good session, yet as we walked out of the meeting hall, we were feeling wan. (Despair is wan-hope in Old English.) Focusing on fear had sucked the life out of us. We began to wonder if we were in a vicious circle—could it be that "driving out fear" actually kept us *in* fear? Was "fear itself" the problem? So we asked ourselves, what if we shifted the conversation to hope, not to negate or invalidate fear, but to introduce some positive energy?

At the time, we were both taking a two-year program in spiritual psychology led by Tom Yeomans of the Concord Institute. This period of research and reflection resulted in our article, "In the Company of Hope,"[3] which is still the foundation of our thinking. Then we defined hope as *an act that generates movement toward a shared, desirable future.* Based on the available research and literature and our own experience in and around organizations, we called out five principles of hope—principles we expand and refine in this volume and attach directly to leadership.

1. Possibility—hopeful goals stretch us yet remain possible.
2. Agency—hopeful engagement requires us to have both a stake in the outcome and the wherewithal to make a difference.
3. Worth—hope concerns what is truly important, not that which is trivial, grandiose, or immoral.
4. Openness—hope thrives on the expectancy of the unknown, on potential, and on spiritual elbow room.
5. Connection—hope attracts companionship and a shared orientation toward reality.

Since 1992, we've remained passionately involved with hope as a professional pursuit, and yet not very surprisingly there are very personal sides to our story as well. In this regard we are no different from "the astonishing majority of humankind" in Reynolds Price's phrase, "capable of turning their own hopeful eyes onto someone else's solitary pain and acting to ease it."[4]

BARBARA'S STORY

I have always considered myself a "glass-half-full" kind of person—feet firmly planted on the ground thanks to my Greek and Midwestern roots. Life is an experience to be fully lived and learned from, every day. Everything happens for a reason. When Harry and I wrote our initial article, I was also a breast cancer survivor, and so I felt I personally knew a thing or two about hope.

Life had deeper lessons for me. The form they took was that dreaded phone call in the middle of the night received in the fall of 1995—a reckless driver had killed my extraordinary 30-year-old son and daughter-in-law. This is not a book about coping with the loss of a child, yet it is, because on that night, in learning the meaning of despair, I began to truly learn the meaning of hope.

As I started to prepare for reentry, I knew I had little body armor if also greater empathy. I couldn't imagine going back to consulting that had been, frankly, too rooted in the tradition of the "deficit model," fixing what was wrong. I had to find a way to bring my skills to work that was more positive, generative, and hopeful.

And so for the last ten years, it has been my joy to lead teams on voyages of discovery into their customers' worlds. It is hopeful work: we uncover possibilities, and we free people from the confines of narrow roles to think strategically and creatively; they learn to trust their intuition, they find and strengthen their voice, and they have an experience of coming together across boundaries to make things happen.

I cannot, nor would I want to, separate myself from my work. Nobody does. What excites me is that hope is everywhere. It just needs an invitation, a context that allows us to bring our full humanity to the table.

HARRY'S STORY

Barbara and I have been on a life's journey together. Although no one would mistake one of us for the other—I'm the tall and bald one, just to state the obvious—there's no getting around a common connection. Our connection is not the coincident fact that we were both born in University Hospital, Iowa City, Iowa, way back when. Our connection is this thing called hope.

In the early 1990s, I was completing a second tour of duty in a multinational corporation as an organizational development and human resources person. Barbara and I met in the town where we both lived, and we had begun working and studying together—we were both interested in building organizational community at the crossroads of TQM (Total Quality Management) and spiritual psychology. Fifteen years into my corporate career, I was feeling itchy and unfulfilled. So in the mid-1990s, I made a move to one of the hot startups of that era—a global company in information technology. The work was difficult—there were twenty-five countries in the mix with too few of us to get it all done, and we were a poorly aligned management team to boot. My job did not play well enough to my strengths, yet I soldiered on.

Then, in a compressed period of time, my wife, daughter, and son experienced personal crises—illness, major surgery, unplanned leaves from schools, and emergency hospitalizations. We all made it through those difficult days, and today my family is wiser and closer, alert and alive. I'm living my calling as a consultant, helping shape realistic and humane workplaces. In my experience, the source of hope is as likely to be suffering as success.

The social psychologist Karl Weick once observed that careers are eccentric, fortuitous, discontinuous, and open to being understood only after the fact,[5] that is, *in retrospect*. Simply put, Barbara and I want hope to work for more people more often and in more places, for their careers, families, organizations, and communities—*in prospect*. That would be pulling the future out of the closet.

HOPE TODAY

Is hope a factor in today's world? Two current best-selling works of science writing concluded that the world is making progress (or not, and there's room for debate about what constitutes progress), and that we're not getting any happier. Richard Layard, who is both a well-known economist and a member of the British House of Lords, has drawn lessons from psychology, sociology, neuroscience, philosophy, as well as economics, and concluded that people in Western societies, though richer, are in no way happier. Crime, depression, and addictions are growing at alarming rates.[6] Gregg Easterbrook, a noted writer and editor, and a visiting fellow in economics at the Brookings Institution, tells us that the percentage of people who describe themselves as being happy in the United States, Japan, and Western Europe has remained the same for fifty years, even as life has grown "fantastically better."[7] Both Layard and Easterbrook make compelling arguments about what should be done, and their books deserve to be read.

Our argument scales down from the world at large and suggests that organizations of every size and type could also use more happiness, and that there is a strong case for hope to help leaders bring that about. Hope, after all, is talked about all the time. A recent Google search yielded more than 146 million references for hope and definitions in all major languages including Chinese, Japanese, Arabic, and Hebrew. Newspaper headlines that reference hope (they appear daily and in all sections of the paper) add local color to the variety of hope's applications:

> "Some Ran and Others Rolled, But All Were Driven by Hope"[8] (the Hope and Possibilities Five Mile Run/Walk in Central Park)

> "A New Hope for Dreams Suspended by Segregation"[9] (Virginia is providing scholarships to students whose careers were cut short by racist school closings in the 1950s)

> "Ray of Hope is Blasted"[10] (Devil Rays beat the Red Sox)

> "Hope and Gloom Out West"[11] (The American West, named by Wallace Stegner as "the native home of hope," is ambivalent about environmentalism)

> "Hearts heavy but hopeful"[12] (mourning the death of Pope John Paul II)

"Those who stutter find hope"[13] (a new device inserted in the ear helps stutterers)

"Tracing a 20-Year Odyssey Across Hope and Despair"[14] (a review of the documentary film "Tarnation")

"Hope's Haven"[15] (a Chinese tiger named Hope is released in South Africa)

"Business Plan: First, You Hope"[16] (New Orleans business assesses damage after Katrina)

"Listen: The Sound of Hope"[17] (on cochlear implants)

"Growing Up in Appalachia Between Hope and Despair"[18] (television review of a PBS documentary)

"Female Boxer Offers Hope to a New Mexico Town Short of Heroes"[19] (fighter battles family history in a troubled town)

"Hoping for Hope"[20] (commentary on the State of the Union Address)

In fact, every branch of the arts, the humanities, and religion, and every field of social science can point to hope (or its more limited companion: optimism) as a theme, an operating principle, a virtue, a value.

Hope is as ancient as humanity, yet it seems inchoate, at least compared with faith and love. Faith, rooted in the past, appears strong and wise, while love makes its powerful presence known in our daily lives. But hope, concerned with things that haven't yet happened, is akin to wishing, waiting, expecting, and dreaming—it retains an element of passivity, mystery, and vexation.

Even the defining story of Pandora is ambiguous, as Thomas Bulfinch, an influential interpreter of Greek mythology, made plain in the nineteenth century.[21] The better-known story has it that Jupiter made Pandora, the first woman, and sent her to earth to be Epimetheus's companion as a punishment for stealing fire from heaven. Pandora was a beautiful creature whose designed-in curiosity got the better of her, and when she opened a strange jar she let lose all manner of diseases and evils. All that remained in the jar was hope. Another version of the story, more probable according to Bulfinch, is that what escaped from the jar were the couple's marriage blessings, gifts from the gods. So which is it? And what does it mean? Is hope the loyal defender against malaise? Is it just another form of grief, like all the others, except that it's the one that didn't get away? Or is it a precious jewel, everlasting symbol of divine care? Really now, can hope be put to work?

Hope is not what it appears at first glance by most people—"most people" can barely agree as to what it really is. This is because hope is complex. Hope maps to human complexity, to our brains, to our lived experience, to our organizational forms, and to the fundamental process of civilization we call leadership. Note that when people in positions of authority offer optimism, while their would-be followers want hope, there is no leadership. Our aim is to bring understanding to hope and hope to leadership, and the job we've assigned ourselves is to arrive at some clarity, introduce some fresh views, and make some suggestions. Beyond this, let's let hope take it from there.

OUR METHOD

The hope field is admittedly in its infancy as a focus for social science. Max De Pree, chairman emeritus of Herman Miller, Inc, and author of *Leadership Is an Art*, says: "Over the years I can't recall reading in any management or leadership books anything about the organizational function of hope."[22]

In 1992, our research method included a cross-disciplinary review of the available literature that yielded underlying principles, which we then applied to organizational settings. In this project, we tested the original model by surveying new material and performing ethnographic research—we asked managers and associates in businesses and nonprofits about their everyday experience of hope. (All quotations, unless otherwise noted, come from our interviews.) Through interviews and reading we've become keenly aware of how people talk about and measure hope. There are many literatures and languages of hope with little agreement as to what is intrinsic. One comprehensive survey offers a fair assessment: hope remains problematic, and consensus is rare.[23]

Perhaps the most promising line of inquiry is that advanced by those who would create "vocabularies of hope … in all shapes and sizes—theories, ethnographies, case studies, vignettes, empirical data, personal narratives, rhetorical speeches, stories told in the classroom, boardroom, or around the kitchen table."[24] As we will show, hope merits all these forms of communication—hope eludes definition, frustrates our needs for closure, tantalizes us with possibility, and ultimately rewards our effort and interest.

BOOK OVERVIEW

This is as much a book about leadership, written *from* hope as it is a book *about* hope written for leaders. Here is the distinction: As organizational practitioners, of course we care about getting "hope" right, but we care much more about helping people work together in ways that serve the greater good. It is our hope that work, workers, and workplaces can be aligned to achieve human worth; we see leadership as the prime mover. For us, hope is the way, not the goal.

Putting Hope to Work is organized in three sections. We begin with "Choosing Hope," where we reveal how people describe their experience of hope at work as well as what is being learned from hope research projects across many disciplines. We conclude the section with a chapter that makes important distinctions among such topics as optimism and wishful thinking as well as denial and fear. Each chapter delineates implications for leadership.

The second section, "Hope's Five Principles," lays out hope's underpinnings and provides case examples to bring them to life. We present a scale based on these principles and other tools that can raise awareness of the status of hope in an organization. Our underlying assumption conforms to the golden mean—strong hope, we argue, derives from having moderate positions on all five principles.

In the third and final section, "Leading from Hope," we describe who hopeful leaders are, what they do, and how they keep hope alive. In our view, hopeful leadership is good leadership—with some specific twists. In the concluding chapter, we restate major themes and offer general suggestions for how to be hopeful about hope.

One of the lessons we learned from Tom Yeomans is the value of holding both ends of an argument in our minds at once—a seeming polarity or an outright contradiction—in order to break out of either/or thinking. Hope is replete with similar puzzles. Friedrich Nietzsche, the nineteenth-century German philosopher who believed in affirming the life we live in as opposed to a world beyond, described hope as both the "worst of evils" and a "greater stimulant of life than any realized joy." So does hope help or hurt in the here-and-now? Then there are imponderables such as hoping in vain, having hopeless hope, and being beyond hope. To get our minds around all this we've needed to hold both sides on many levels of meaning and to think "both/and."

In our basic approach to hope, we believe *both* in the value of social constructivism, which is a theory of language proposing that "words themselves can create worlds,"[25] *and* in the notion that hope is core to human nature. It is social constructivist to understand hope as a "state" and to search for meaning in how people talk about hope, for changed talk changes outcomes. And yet we also see hope as having hardwired, "trait" dimensions: hope is on the list of "human universals" compiled by the anthropologist Donald Brown,[26] hope has been nominated by the philosopher Peter Geach as one of the "basic modern virtues,"[27] and hope is categorized by the psychologists Christopher Peterson and Martin E.P. Seligman as one of the twenty-four character strengths and virtues in human nature.[28] We cut it down the middle and so for us, hope is at point five in the grand scheme of things: half what we do, half who we are.

To slice it differently and repurpose a distinction made by the anthropologist Clifford Geertz, hope is *both* "blink" *and* "wink."[29] Having a "special connection with the brain,"[30] hope can be interpreted *both* as an involuntary, adaptive behavior that clears the eye, *and* as intentional and deliberate eye contact. Hope works in *both* automatic *and* conscious modes, at the crossroads of thinking, feeling, and doing.

Dr. Jerome Groopman's description of the biology of hope underscores how mind and body "interplay"—that is, signals from the body cause changes in the structure of the brain, whereas thoughts and feelings alter the body itself.[31] Virtuous cycles are created where conscious hoping soothes pain while the lessening of pain evokes hopeful thoughts and feelings—one process feeds the other in rounds of expanding joy. At the interpersonal level, with which we are mainly concerned, the question embedded in everything we say in this book is this: *How can leaders initiate hopeful, virtuous cycles within their organizations and accelerate positive results?*

Section One

Choosing Hope

You have the power to choose hope. And you choose giving hope to people. That's the secret of leadership. Nothing complicated. You don't have to take a test; you just have to meet the test of life.[1]

Peter Koestenbaum

The evidence is mounting—hope is real, and it works. Even if there were evidence to the contrary, it would probably make very little difference to us in our daily lives. Every day is a new day for hope, and that in itself is cause for hope. Still it's good to know that science is coming to our side, and that we can "choose hope" to make things better in our individual lives and our places of work.

Hope is older than language and as old as human memory, and yet the first scientific wake-up call was sounded in 1959, at an annual meeting of the American Psychiatric Association. In a now-famous address, Karl Menninger, MD, founder and dean of the Menninger School of Psychiatry and winner of the Presidential Medal of Freedom, presented his colleagues with this challenge:

"Our shelves hold many books now on the place of faith in science and psychiatry, and on the vicissitudes of man's efforts to love and be loved. But when it comes to hope, our shelves are bare. The journals are silent. The Encyclopaedia Britannica devotes many columns to the topic of love, and many more to faith. But hope, poor little hope! She is not even listed.

"... Are we not now duty bound to speak up as science, not about a new rocket or a new fuel or a new bomb or a new gas, but about this

ancient but rediscovered truth, the validity of Hope in human development,—Hope, alongside of its immortal sisters, Faith and Love."[2]

Whether or not Menninger deserves credit, hope began to get its scientific
due in the 1960s. Erik Erikson, the developmental psychologist, related hope
to basic trust and mistrust among infants at the beginning of the life cycle,
calling attention to both its biological and spiritual importance.[3] Jerome
Frank, MD, a professor of psychiatry at Johns Hopkins, having done research
based on a grant from the National Institute of Mental Health, reported
there is cumulative evidence that, "Hope inspires a feeling of well being
and is a spur to action."[4] Also in the 1960s, Ezra Stotland produced the
first cognitive-behavioral book on the psychology of hope, showing how it
can be treated pragmatically and without interference from religious or
cultural leanings.[5]

The first scale to measure hope was published in 1974 by Louis
Gottschalk, opening the way to empirically quantifiable measures of
hope that continue to be developed and refined to this day.[6] Converting
hope into a numerical value enables psychological studies that might predict outcomes over a range of human events. C. Rick Snyder, a psychologist who was specifically encouraged by Menninger to "place thinking at
the core of hope rather than emotions"[7] developed his hope scale
in 1991—which we will refer to in Chapter 3 when we relate evidence
of hope's rewards. Snyder has also led the way in applying the concepts
of hope to children.[8]

In 1985, Karin Dufault and Benita Martoccchio published an influential
paper in the nursing literature using participant observation of elderly cancer
patients over two years; they developed a process-oriented definition of hope
consisting of six dimensions: affective, cognitive, behavioral, affiliative, temporal, and contextual. They found among other things that hope and hopelessness can indeed coexist, and their work has encouraged many more
qualitative and ethnographic studies.[9]

In 1990, James Averill, George Catlin, and Kyum Koo Chon published
their study of hope's "rules" based on analysis of the language of hope. Their
work included Korean students, and it opened up cross-cultural studies of
hope. In the following year, Martin E.P. Seligman, who later became president of American Psychological Association, published an optimistic book
on optimism that has become the founding argument for positive psychology. In the text, Seligman includes an optimism test that also yields a score
for hope. Hopefulness, in terms of the precepts of learned optimism, means
we reject "permanent and universal" causes for our misfortunes and can
explain away our troubles as being temporary ("I'm just having a bad
day—life happens") and specific ("That was a dumb answer I just gave—
I'm really not a stupid person."). "No other single score is as important as
your hope score," he says.[10]

One of the most extensive efforts at cross-cultural, ethnographic research was performed by the nursing researcher and theorist Rosemarie Rizzo Parse and her team, conducted in nine countries and over four years during the 1990s. Their investigation into the "lived experience of hope" suggests both universal principles as well as highly individual stories.[11] By now, hope research is beginning to thrive in the sciences, making up distance between them and the disciplines of philosophy, religion, history, social criticism, and the arts, which have always been in the hope game. Hope research is even being institutionalized: the Hope Foundation of Alberta, "dedicated to the study and advancement of hope," has specific missions related to service, training, education, and research.

There's more research about hope in the works. Patricia Bruininks, winner of the 2005 Seligman award for outstanding dissertation research in positive psychology, is one of the newest scholars of hope. Her recent findings are pushing her "to go beyond global measures of hope to investigate how individual differences, beliefs, and situational variables affect the 'ups and downs' of hoping."[12] So the history of hope will continue to lengthen. Studs Terkel writes in his oral history of hope, quoting a retired farm worker, that you just can't lose hope, because "Hope dies last."[13]

BUILDING ON STRENGTHS

Research in organizational health rests on the models that dominate how we understand and investigate physical and mental health, and these continue to be rooted in the "3 D's": disease, deficit, and dysfunction. A survey of thirty years of psychological publications cited in an address in 1998 by Martin E.P. Seligman, counted 46,000 papers on depression, and a meager 400 on joy. He said that "social science now finds itself in almost total darkness about the qualities that make life most worth living."[14] At about the same time, a group of senior researchers performed a thorough review of articles and books on hope and "found not one contribution from the management and organizational sciences."[15]

In the last ten years, however, evidence of a move away from the "3 Ds" toward a more positive model of describing and appreciating both individual and collective behavior can be seen in disciplines as diverse as philosophy, psychology, biology, organizational behavior, and in particular, healthcare. The focus and momentum of research, writing, and practice is shifting toward what's right and what's working: from disease to health, from deficit to abundance, and from dysfunction to optimal performance.

The essence of this approach is "building on strengths" rather than finding faults and failings or measuring people against normative averages. Human beings can't be "averaged," after all—when you have your head in an oven and your feet in the freezer, your body temperature may be 98.6 degrees *on average*, and of course you'll likely be dead! Building a strengths-based enterprise, where people can show their best and be challenged for more, where the safety and health of everyone is a priority, and where all who belong want to belong, is the hard work of organizational hope.

The handbook and classification of character strengths and virtues compiled by Christopher Peterson, Martin E.P. Seligman, and forty of their colleagues promises to take the positive approach to building the good life to another level.[16] Working across history and cultures and "leaving no stone unturned," the team has identified six core virtues and twenty-four character strengths that exist in human nature—and that can be harnessed in the service of "the good life." This is an enormous undertaking that will remain work in progress for years, but already it is having an effect. In leadership coaching, teambuilding, and organizational development activities, the identification of individual strengths offers positive solutions where before there were problems, and hope where there was hurt.

Hope with its "synonyms," optimism, future-mindedness, and future orientation, stands as one of the twenty-four signature strengths. Individuals who are strong in hope strongly agree with statements such as the following:

- I always look on the bright side.
- I believe good will triumph over evil.
- I expect the best.
- I have a plan.
- I know I will succeed.

Interestingly, hope and optimism are considered "Velcro constructs" in the handbook because all manner of strengths seem to correlate with them for unknown reasons.[17] This leads us to acknowledge the utter complexity of hope—and to applaud its being that way.

MANY MEANINGS, TWO THEMES

Jaklin Eliott's extensive summary of the hope literature concludes with the statement, "Hope is, or can be, positive, negative, divine, secular, interpersonal, individual, social, ideological, inherent, acquired, objective, subjective, a practice, a possession, an emotion, a cognition, true, false, enduring, transitory, measured, defined, inspired, learnt ... and the list goes on." Though there is now an "explosion of hope," according to Eliott, it's difficult to predict where we will go next with hope. Agreement about its definition approaches the same degree of probability as agreement as to the meaning of human nature—"hope's a slippery little concept," she says. Nevertheless, according to Eliott, two themes pull through and endure: hope's significance and hope's power.[18]

"It just occurred to me that it would be even <u>more</u> hellish if we left them just a little bit of hope."

Our intention is to help make hope easier to grasp in settings that lack hopeful vocabularies. Any questions we had about hope's power and significance when we started this project have been completely resolved by the people we've listened to and observed in action. The conceptual framework we've developed brings together lessons of others that helps create patterns where now there are only data points. Our prediction is that hope will continue to attract scientific attention and extend its reach into the study and practice of leadership.

THE VERTICAL AND THE HORIZONTAL

One of the confusions we've encountered in our many conversations concerns whether hope is really only about personal salvation, the coming apocalypse, or the end of history, and whether hoping is the exclusive province of true believers, be they secular or sacred. This view would say hope is a matter of predicting the worst and throwing ourselves at the mercy of a higher power. We hope, therefore, in order to save ourselves when all else fails, because all else *will* fail. This "vertical" version of hope is concerned with going "up" to paradise/personal success, or "down" to the underworld/personal failure. It can be a fatalistic and individualistic kind of hope, radical in the extreme.[19] For many people who don't hold these views but suspect that hope is somehow implicated in a form of fatalism, hoping is a big turnoff.

Here's where we stand. For us, hope is "horizontal"—it is always about freedom, about alternatives, and about being with other people. Hope doesn't predict; it gives options. Hope doesn't determine outcomes; it offers choices and helps us achieve what we truly want. We choose hope to help us make better choices about most other things.

An old Cherokee Indian was teaching his grandchildren about life. He said to them:

A fight is going on inside me. It is a terrible fight, and it is between two wolves. One wolf represents fear, anger, envy, sorrow, regret, greed, arrogance, self-pity, guilt, resentment, inferiority, lies, false pride, superiority, ego, and unfaithfulness. The other wolf stands for joy, peace, love, hope, sharing, serenity, humility, kindness, forgiveness, benevolence, friendship, empathy, generosity, truth, compassion and faithfulness. This same fight is going on inside you and inside every other person too.

They thought about it for a minute, and then one child asked his grandfather,

Which wolf will win, grandfather?

The old Cherokee simply replied,

The one you feed.

Chapter 1

The Signs of Hope at Work

Anyone who has looked Hope in the face will never forget it. He will search for it everywhere he goes, among all kinds of men. And he will dream of finding it again someday, somewhere, perhaps among those closest to him.[1]

Octavio Paz

Pretend for a moment that you are an anthropologist from Mars. Walk into your organization as if for the first time. You are here to do observational research. You are looking for clues, cues, patterns that reveal whether hope is at work. What do you notice? What gets your attention? We invite you to fine-tune your senses and look with fresh eyes at your familiar landscape—for tracks of hope. This is what David Malone, a former Chief Procurement Officer for the City of Chicago, would look for:

"Hope is a human emotion that manifests itself in words and actions, so in order to ascertain a relative 'HQ' (Hope Quotient) for an organization, it might serve us best to look for human signals rather than typical business signals. Human signals are things like attendance, tardiness, overtime w/o pay, positive attitudes and contribution, loyalty and optimism. Some of these are simple and measurable and yet others are subjective in nature. It's important however to have all of the sensors turned on for these characteristics because they are the emotions that either drive or inhibit performance. The rest is simply process and technology."

Tracking hope is an exercise involving all your senses, your intuition as well as your logic. Hope may be explicit and even named by those who experience it, or it may be lurking behind the scenes, unacknowledged yet exerting influence. In the words of anthropologist Edward T. Hall, "Those of us who keep our eyes open can read volumes in what we see going on around us."[2] Here are the observations of a manager who attends to hope:

> "You know that hope is present because you can feel it emotionally, physically, spiritually and intellectually. It isn't something easily described, but you can feel it at the very core of your being. You can see and experience it in others. Hope is authentic and can't be faked. It shows up in how you and people act, in what is done, in what is said. You can observe it in a presentation, in meetings, and in how people interact. You can see it in the written word by reading in between the lines."

From our in-depth conversations with leaders around the world, we learned that while many know what hope looks like, sounds like, and feels like in the context of their work and workplace, few think "in terms of hope." According to Sarah Osmer, a Director at Starbucks Coffee Company, "I'm struck by how rarely I use the word, but how true it is to my work and why I stay connected here."

What's going on? Why does the language of hope hide its head while the impact and signs of hope are there to be read? Perhaps, as Rabbi Maurice Lamm says, "We know in our bones hope is everything. In the back of our minds we suspect it is nothing at all."[3] This chapter begins our exploration of hope in terms of language and action. Why don't we talk (seriously) about it? Are we sure it's really there?

A TALE OF TWO MEETINGS

Have a seat at the table in two actual meetings—the names of the players and their firms are being withheld—and witness hope (or its lack) at work.

Meeting One

The speakerphone is in its usual place at the center of the conference table, and we're connected to three other states. It's the weekly meeting of the management board of a Midwestern medical products firm, and the president is driving the agenda. He's known for being a demanding manager from whom "you will learn a lot." On this day, the demands are in full force—what we're learning is how to please the boss.

> *And while I stood there I saw more than I can tell and I understood more than I saw.*
>
> *Black Elk*

The president was recruited from a well-known medical products corporation nearby by a group of venture capitalists to rebuild this small firm, and then sell it. The "VCs" are disappointed, however—they paid too much for an old company that needs more help over a longer period of time than they had wagered. Their standard management approach is to hire tough operators and then turn up the pressure. They brook no excuses.

So here we are, a dozen of us, cast together. There's the head of operations recruited from yet another large and successful medical products company; the general counsel, newly hired from a prestigious law firm; a head of research and development with patents under his name; a talented and aggressive young finance director; a quality manager who knows his stuff and who just left a bad situation with a similar firm; a sales manager with a successful track record who is moving in from another state with his family; and a human resources manager.

The meeting today concerns "Lean" manufacturing processes being introduced in the factories. Consultants are hard at work, training operators to redesign their routines to reduce time and increase quality. Lean manufacturing is a methodology invented by Toyota to improve performance by becoming a "learning enterprise." Here the emphasis is on reducing costs—jobs are at stake, and the workers know it. In fact, the consultants will be paid according to how much cost can be taken out of the system, regardless of the consequences for people or company culture.

The first rule of Toyota's production system, the "Toyota Way," is, "Base your management decisions on a long-term philosophy, even at the expense of short-term financial goals." We're violating this rule.

The meeting format is to "drill down" into details, person by person. It's a hub-and-spoke method: the president as grand inquisitor. And so, when it's not our turn to be questioned, we stay out of the way. To offer support to a colleague in a meeting like this is asking for trouble. We share a sense of dread that trouble will come our way no matter what, and we feel tense, noncollaborative, strangely compliant. We're running late, and we're off the agenda; it's warm in the room, and there are no windows to open.

The products in question are high-quality life-saving instruments. This could or should be a feel-good firm. Both the people freshly recruited to run the business, as well as the longtimers in the factories and labs, are hard working and hopeful that the business can make it. The truth, however, is that we're not "feeling good."

Within the year, the heads of operations, sales, quality, and human resources will be fired. Many others will lose their jobs or leave, and sites will be closed. The company will underperform against the owners' expectations. The headquarters will be moved, and the company name will be changed, superficial changes with no effect. People will continue to work enormous hours and feel the heat. The company will continue to limp along. And the president will be replaced.

Meeting Two

Five miles away, at another company in the same town, it's the end of a long day, and we're in full conference-room mode: oval table cluttered with projector, water bottles, and laptops; walls covered with diagrams, action items, and brainstormed ideas; flipcharts and briefcases on the floor surrounding us on all sides. There are fifteen of us: visiting factory managers, quality improvement experts known as "Black Belts," and consultants versed in organizational culture and change. We're clustering around a speakerphone connected to several factory locations.

It's a working meeting containing both promise and peril—the objective is to help site leaders deploy their "Six Sigma" improvement projects with greater urgency and effectiveness—Six Sigma is a management approach adopted by such corporations as General Electric and AlliedSignal to increase performance using standardized methods and rigorous analyses of data. The promise is in the potential cost savings. The peril is in coming up with too little, too late, to satisfy customers, investors, and senior managers.

We're on a company campus that bears witness to both peril and promise. Our building is the last company structure in what was once a square mile of multistory brick factories and offices, in its time a thriving industrial complex. By now, half of the old buildings have been razed, and most of the others are vacant or owned by public agencies and other companies. All around us is evidence that there are serious consequences when we don't get it right.

Yet our building is a hive of energy and enthusiasm. The offices are "open concept," and the workforce is a multinational mix of employees engaged in growing a truly global business—managing the retail apparel supply chain from factories as far-flung as China, Honduras, and Turkey for world's largest retail companies and clothing manufacturers.

By design, the group has been exchanging views—telling the unvarnished truth about what's really working and what's not. There's a low level of anxiety and a high level of energy. Some of the targets are reachable—but just barely.

The heart of the meeting is the time spent by each plant manager and Black Belt thinking partner as they inquire into the actual lived situation of two of their peers from another plant. They ask, what's the story? How do you know that's really the case? What's helping and what's in the way? And most important, can we help you with our resources, best practices, or even just moral support? It's "real work in real time." Now it's time to debrief the day. What do we say? We do a "go-around" and listen to each person:

"It's helpful to meet colleagues from other divisions and build a network."

"I'm glad to refresh my memory of the Six Sigma tools and how they can be used."

"This meeting takes away some of the fear associated with learning and using new tools."

"I feel less alone."

"I've gotten some great ideas today, and I'm making new friends."

"It's always useful to step back from the daily grind and gain some perspective—in a safe environment."

Then, unbidden and as natural as can be, there is this final voice:

"I feel hope."

WHEN WE DON'T TALK HOPE

One of our earliest surprises as ethnographers of hope was that many people had never connected the word "hope" with the word "work." Organizations talk about morale, engagement, retention, innovation, vision, inspirational and transformational leadership, learning, potential, emotional intelligence, values ... and the list goes on. These are the acceptable terms, a little "softer" than profit and loss, yet they fall within the linguistic comfort zone. Hope may lie at the core of these concepts and processes, yet still the connection is not made, at least not at the outset. The overwhelming first response when we asked people about hope in their organizations was, "I never thought about it in terms of our business." At its strongest, this reluctance to "talk hope" verged on taboo; at its most mundane it was simply not connected with an understanding of how organizations work. Why not?

Is Hope Too Wishy-Washy?

"We don't talk hope because we love predictability and measures," we were told by an executive. 'Hope suggests vagueness.' Chief Executives are unlikely to tell analysts or their workforces or even their friends, "We hope next quarter's results will be better." As one CEO told us:

"Hope has a negative connotation here—and so it's never been used. Hope brings ambiguity and conditions—we don't have room for that. It doesn't fit. Hope is not an emotion we want in the business...."

According to another executive:

"We talk about dreams—we dream ambitiously—more than hope."

And a third:

> "Hope is not spoken. We talk limitations, barriers."

And one more (a man):

> "I never thought of this work in terms of hope. This is not a language leaders, especially men, are comfortable with."

Rabbi Maurice Lamm has observed how the word, hope "slips unnoticed into our speech" so often it has become "a mindless, throwaway truism."[4]

> "Traditionally, it has been the province of preachers and politicians, not scientists—and certainly not managers."

The challenge for leaders is to "remember" hope and what it can do without appearing feckless.

Does Hope Belong Here?

Applying the language of hope to the workplace just didn't work for some. Several disconnections were especially pronounced. The first came from the belief that hope is primarily a spiritual concept and as such is "kind of a heavy word—more serious, more fundamental." As one person told us:

> "I drew a blank at first because I don't associate the two— hope and work. For me, there's a deep element of spirituality [in hope] disconnected from the workplace."

For some, hope is strong language for the workplace. For others it's too weak—"hope is on the shy side of faith" as one manager defines it. We were told that "hope doesn't apply to the business world; it's for individuals."

They ask for definitions.

The academics that is.
The scholars muse
And the theologians struggle
The linguists quibble
And the philosophers argue
And all remain puzzled.
The single mom
The dying patient
The person with MS who can no longer
*   make his limbs move*
They don't ask for definitions.
He will tell you
The nurse says it with compassion,
And her grandmother sang it with
*   her eyes.*
His mother cries it with every tear
And her brother tied it to a tree.
They know it in their souls.
And none are puzzled.

*   Ronna Fay Jevne*

We were also told that hope is really about what we do for others. Dr. Zeda Rosenberg, CEO of the International Partnership for Microbicides, an organization whose mission is to stop the transmission of HIV Aids in our lifetime, says, "Hope comes in because you're helping people, making the world safer, making the quality and length of life better. Help and hope are intertwined." Similarly, for Dr. David Hohn, President and CEO of Roswell Park Cancer Institute in Buffalo, New York, the world's first cancer center, hope is superceded by faith:

> "I don't spend time thinking about my own need for hope. I do think about creating it for others. I am driven to facilitate scientific breakthroughs that give reason for others to have hope of being cured. With 75% of children surviving their cancers and increasing control of cancer in adults, there is every reason to have hope."

At Roswell Park, we face every day standing on faith that progress will continue.

Roswell Park's website says that until cancer is cured, "Hope inspires our vision at RPCI: to be the best...." When help and hope are entwined in people's minds, hope belongs more to what is accomplished for clients and customers than to how the work is performed.

How About "Hopes"?

The most organizationally acceptable form of "hope talk" is the concept of shared hopes. A manager explained that "*Hopes* is a unifying spirit, the focus of our attention." Sometimes, hopes are consolidated in dreams or vision: "Hope has many names: call it vision, a belief in what you're trying to accomplish."

Creating an organizational vision or mission, then, legitimizes hope talk. According to Bain and Company, a strategic consulting firm, a vision statement "describes the desired future position of the company," and the visioning process requires leaders to:

- clearly identify the corporate culture, values, strategy, and view of the future by interviewing employees, suppliers, and customers;
- address the commitment the firm has to its key stakeholders, including customers, employees, shareholders, and communities;
- ensure that the objectives are measurable, the approach is actionable, and the vision is achievable;
- communicate the message in clear, simple, and precise language;
- develop buy-in and support throughout the organization.[5]

Thus vision statements can contain multiple hopes, preferably ones that are measurable, actionable, and achievable, and the process of arriving at organizational buy-in is itself a principle of hope. Creating a vision and having hopes is an important step in the journey of putting hope to work.

OUTWARD AND VISIBLE SIGNS

Charles Handy describes an organization with spirit and soul in much the same way as those we interviewed described the hopeful organization. You can see it and feel it when you walk in the door or when you meet someone who works there. There is an abundance of what he calls "E" factors: "energy, enthusiasm, effort, excitement, excellence, and so on." The talk is in first-person plural, and the organization is about something besides making money, "something grander, something worthy of one's commitment, skills, and time."[6] If hope is indeed "a primary source of positive knowledge and action in organizational life,"[7] as three social scientists at Case Western Reserve University have posited, then it follows that hope must be evident in how people appear, what they say, and how they work.

How People Appear

The eyes are the window to the soul, according to the adage, so they must also be a window into hope. In the language of one observant manager:

> "I know by the light that sits behind someone's eyes. Instead of nodding yes, they're thinking yes."

People spoke of the eyes "coming alive" or getting bigger. From the eyes, hope moves to "the whole face, animated, coming to life." The voice too, comes to life "with energy and passion—no flat emotional tone." In fact, the whole body is energized. As one leader who had succeeded in rescuing a business said:

> "You can physically see it—the spring in a person's step. When I first came to this organization, people were beaten down, ignored, victims—no hope. Now they've started smiling again, laughing, not that tight look on their faces."

According to one of our straight-talking respondents, "Hope in a company either is there or it is not. When it is, you can see it in your people in their attitude, behavior, work ethic, on their faces, in their language, in their eyes, in their step." This is hope's silent, behavioral language.

What People Say

As you walk the halls, stand at the coffee machine, or sit in a meeting (or more likely, as you leave a meeting), listen closely for the level of positive talk;

it is a key indicator of whether hope is alive and well. Our respondents describe positive talk as being confident, can-do, forward-looking, inclusive of people and ideas, tolerant, energetic, realistic, and honest. Here is one manager's statement:

"People speak of and act on proactive and positive endeavors they would not have considered possible some time before. They speak about the future and what they want to make it better."

There is a greater willingness to do whatever is needed: "No complaining about working harder—get the job done. People have a high level of personal commitment because they know they can make a difference." This isn't simply Pollyanna's optimism; most workplaces are far too demanding and stressful for her cheerful outlook alone to make the difference. True positive talk, in good or bad times, indicates true hope.

On the other hand, true negative talk indicates true hopelessness. For example, we were told how in one unhappy work environment, "We used to focus on what we couldn't be/do. Excuses were embedded in the culture." Zander and Zander call such "downward spiral talk ... a resigned way of speaking that excludes possibility ... [and] tells us compellingly how things are going from bad to worse."[8] Psychologists call hopeless talk "pessimistic rumination," the tendency to be trapped by negative thoughts and emotions.

Upward spiral talk, on the other hand, is expansive, freeing, and often metaphorical. We heard of many allusions to hope's nourishing and life-enhancing qualities, often related to water: a deep well, a reservoir, a spring. In 1990, an academic research team scoured the literature of hope and conducted interviews with students to capture and classify metaphorical expressions of hope. Hope is the lifeblood of the soul, a sun or a star, pie in the sky, a fragile object, a charlatan, a spur to industry, and so on. Although making no claims as to completeness, they identified 108 distinct metaphors and concluded that, as distinct from metaphors for anger or love, for example, hope language is more expansive.[9] This is an important clue in understanding hope.

A verse by the poet Samuel Taylor Coleridge, one of the best-known metaphors of hope and work, takes us a step further:

"Work without hope draws nectar in a sieve,
And hope without an object cannot live."[10]

Coleridge's image is incomplete, according to Joseph Godfrey, author of a philosophy of hope. He argues that hope is definite in its focus—but not concrete. Hope does not have an *object* or thing to hope for—it has as an *objective* in its line of sight.[11] Thus, to hope for a good boss or a rewarding assignment or an enterprise that has meaning or a business that is successful is to hope for *more than* that these arrangements could exist—it is to hope that *I'll be able to have them.* That's hope for you: personal, pertinent, powerful.

Hope metaphors, understandably open, reflect hope's depth. "Hope has the ability to be fluid in its expectations, and in the event that the desired object or outcome does not occur, hope can still be present."[12] Hope is patient and expectant, confident that it knows what it is doing, without having to commit to an irreversible course of action.

How People Work

Hope at work manifests itself in peoples' attitudes toward their own work and in their interactions with others. What connects the two is a heightened sense of personal commitment and responsibility, not only to me and my job, the "I," but to the whole, the community, the team, the "we." According to Chris Drew, a consultant working with public and nonprofit organizations,

> "Sometimes unprecedented behaviors and patterns emerge, such as speaking with people outside your normal work circle, spending extra (including personal) time on projects, people leading improvement efforts when they used to rely on others to lead, and asking leadership for resources (time, training, money, tools) to build or develop something."

In a laboratory environment, recent research on the behaviors of high-, medium-, and low-performance teams (as measured by profitability, customer satisfaction, and 360-degree evaluations) has revealed patterns that bear directly on hope. The "speech acts" of sixty strategic business unit planning teams were coded, analyzed, and modeled. By way of qualitative observation, high-performance teams were characterized by "an atmosphere of buoyancy" with "emotional spaces that were expansive" with "possibilities for action and creativity." In contrast, low-performance teams showed "lack of support and enthusiasm" matched with "distrust and cynicism." Medium-performance teams were in between.

Computer modeling generated themes with direct practicality for organizations. High performance in teams is a function of three dynamics: a balance of inquiry and advocacy, a balance of attention given to others with focus on self, and an overweighting on the positive. Thus high-performance (read: hopeful) working groups succeed by expanding emotional space in at least three ways:

1. through dialogue (listening and questioning as well as stating positions);
2. by keeping a balanced perspective (on customers, on stakeholders, and on the world "outside"); and
3. through affirmation and acknowledgement (the ratio of their positive versus negative talk with one another is 5.625:1!)[13]

Bruce Bacon, vice president of human resources at HP Hood dairy operations, captured the essence of the above with a simple image of hope: "It's the door starting to open, instead of the door starting to close."

For Craig Wildrick, an executive vice president at Wells Fargo, hope is present at work when he sees "self-organizing behavior." Craig describes three states of observable behavior that show increasing levels of hope and personal responsibility for the whole:

"Level One: Nobody buys-in; everyone is working a personal agenda.

"Level Two: Some want to get somewhere but don't have any hope things will change.

"Level Three: People start finding ways to solve challenges, getting there without a lot of pushing. Hope generates energy and requires a lot less control and structure. People start talking to each other, seeking solutions. Each cell of the body operates as part of the whole, organized around the health of the whole, choosing how to engage."

Once at Level Three, "We take responsibility for allowing ourselves to be hopeful, we assert ourselves more, become more tolerant and flexible." Craig is describing hope in action, a flexible, dynamic force that helps us overcome difficult challenges and setbacks because, like reality, hope is not static. Hope constantly monitors reality and adjusts expectations accordingly.

When we feel hope our confidence in ourselves and others grows. We know "I" and "We" can make a difference. The signs of hope begin inside us and extend to include those with whom we work—in the words of Jennifer Cassettari, a manager at Bulgari:

"I know when Hope is present when I want to face the day in all its 'dailyness'—but with a sense of greater purpose. I want to accomplish my work—and extend myself to take on a bit more. I want to take care of myself and others—and create an environment of beauty and peace. I want to tend to the needs of the day—and look forward to the future with anticipation. I want to deplore those things that are sad, shabby, and unworthy—and continue to believe that the human spirit is capable of so much more."

A founding member of a group of scholars focusing their research on the positive dimensions of organizational behavior calls hope "the most unique," among positive organizational concepts such as happiness, emotional intelligence, and confidence. Despite its potential impact it has had the least attention.[14] Looking for signs of hope at work is perhaps the best place to start in correcting that pattern.

Chapter 2

The Experience of Hope at Work

We had no <u>reason</u> to expect what happened . . . but we did have hope.[1]
Karl Menninger

In his famous lecture before the American Psychiatric Association in 1959, Karl Menninger noted that the Kansas state hospital program had lived through fifteen years in which psychiatric admissions increased tenfold while the patient population actually decreased—in other words more people were being helped and sent home. The "crucial element" at play in this shift was "the inculcation of hope" in the doctors and all those who helped the patients—in family members, in officials, and in the larger community—and finally in the patients themselves. "We had no *reason* to expect what happened . . . but we did have hope." In fact, said Menninger, they had more than hope: they had had real life *experiences* of hope.[2]

What is the actual experience of hope for people at work? How do they describe what hope feels like? How do they know when it's present? Four broad themes emerged from our conversations that described peoples' experiences of hope at work: energy, belief, reality, and meaning. These four themes intersect and reinforce each other, combining in ways that are difficult to dissect, so we will discuss them one by one.

ENERGY

Once over the language hurdle, people begin telling their stories of hope at work with great enthusiasm. There is a burst of energy that comes just in recalling the circumstances. They talk about a "positive, contagious energy" that spurs people to action. Hope galvanizes and creates a "chain reaction" that reinforces itself by making good things happen. Said one: "Collective hope means there is a contagion that reflects, points out, and savors the things that work." Hope's energy is infectious. In the words of Dr. Menninger, "hope fires hope." It spreads because people are naturally attracted to it and "want to stay close to it." Hope not only lights your fire, it also ripples outward. "Hope is magnetic," says Joe Gottschalk, a senior manager at the Wrigley Company. "You're drawn to it like a bug to a zapper."

It is this energetic aspect of hope that provides the link to action: "Hope underpins action and runs before it."[3] The way to tap this energy is to get up and get going: to help, to lend a hand, to become active—in lighting fires, in tearing down barriers, in achieving small wins, or in actively communicating what you want. Experiencing hope fuels a positive energy to take action toward a desired goal. Jerome Frank, Professor of Psychiatry at Johns Hopkins and a pioneer among therapists in speaking of the role of hope, once described hope as "a spur to action."[4] Anthropologist Lionel Tiger writes that hope is "a hormone of action so necessary, such an obvious element of behavior, that people and communities without it are like water without hydrogen—the physics don't work."[5]

It's important to note that positive energy is not only more productive it's also a lot more enjoyable, a considerable benefit for the people who talked with us. Said one:

> "Hope is more fun. Life is too short for negative energy. We're spending way too much time in the office to be miserable."

The energy of hope is generative, said another:

> "Hope gives you more energy than worry. I can look forward to the start of the week and think 'Oh great!' instead of 'Oh God!' and knowing I'll be dragging myself through the day."

It plays an important role in our resilience, according to a third:

> "When I am hopeful, even though things are not great, I keep my perspective. I'm not as stressed."

The philosopher Luc Bovens argues that hope has both instrumental and intrinsic value.[6] One of hope's *instrumental* values is its ability to counter risk aversion. Daniel Kahneman, the psychologist who won a Nobel Prize in economics, has shown how much people dislike loss—roughly twice as much as they enjoy an equal gain. That is, most people will risk losing a sum of money on the flip of a coin only if they stand to gain double.[7] So, "in a fair gamble," hope helps us focus on the gains and not on the losses, whereas fear does the reverse and fixates us on the dire. Hope is a balance that helps maintain energy. It keeps us from becoming overwhelmed or paralyzed by risk and stress.

One of hope's *intrinsic* values, according to Bovens, is that it provides pleasure—we can imagine better circumstances in the future and this pleasant anticipation both motivates and enables progress. To the degree that we seek authentic happiness, therefore, hope provides energy that influences outcomes.

BELIEF

Hope presents itself as positive energy, yet its driving force is belief, "the presence of positive expectations." It is both a "belief that things *can* happen," as we heard, and the "unshakeable belief that things will continue to evolve for the better." Hopeful belief is different than belief in evidence— it is a commitment to a particular stance that gives guidance to one's life.[8] Hopeful belief represents a choice, not a conclusion based on the evidence.

Organizationally, making the choice to believe, to allow oneself genuine hope in the "name of what is not yet seen," is an enormous act of trust, a belief in leaders, vision, and the ability to execute. For many veterans of dashed hopes, the experience of hoping one more time is not unlike Samuel Johnson's description of a second marriage as "the triumph of hope over experience." Choosing to believe "requires you bear risk," said a manager, "You can't stay guarded."

Marsha Everton, CEO of the Pfaltzgraff Company, led a massive transformation and restructuring of the century-old pottery maker. Along the very difficult way, hope meant "moving one more person over the line to believe."

> "In a turnaround situation the organization is feeling bashed. You need people who have confidence and can change the momentum [and avoid] getting caught in the downward spiral."

Though our beliefs can be externally catalyzed, the ultimate source is internal. The way to access our beliefs and harness their power is to become self-aware and intentional, to be affirming and positive, to be trusting and to orient our thinking toward strengths. "Hope is believing in spite of the evidence, then watching the evidence change."[9] When our belief system gives thumbs up, and the energy of hope kicks in, our whole system— head, heart, and hands—orients itself toward our desired future. Energy and belief, taking action outside ourselves and taking stock inside, thinking and feeling—hope engages us on many levels and in many ways.

When businesses are restructured, downsized, acquired, or divested, there are always downsides for people—losses in comfort and continuity at the very least, but too often there are accompanying losses in pride or pay. We are most interested in how hope can lend a hand during periods of organizational turmoil. Here's a story of a hope-based turnaround as told by Charles Salyer, one of our respondents:

"We entered a corporate atmosphere where hope was gone and fear of the future was the predominant feeling. Revenues were dwindling and people were idle. Who will lose their job? When will the money run out? Who is in charge? What is happening? Why are we trying so hard? Managers were negative. Criticism was the tool of the day. Why did you do it that way? Why is it not done? You can be replaced! The management style was simply, 'what's in it for me?' People just downright hated to go to work.

"The first task was to regain hope. We began each day arriving early and greeting employees at the door. Great to have you here! Beautiful day! Let's knock their socks off today. Let's do a little more today than we did yesterday. Within a week the entire attitude had changed. People were more up beat. Managers took control of their areas. He must know something! The second step was information. We had company meetings with full exposure of the company position. Here is where we are and here is where we are going. We will get there if we work together. There is no doubt, we can do it.

"Gone was the focus on losses. Gone was the focus on errors and mistakes. The focus returned to the job instead of fear. We started each company meeting with each person stating something positive that had happened the prior week. In the beginning these examples were thin. Then the miraculous happened. Small successes were championed. Mistakes were turned into 'what we learned.' A major issue became, 'well we know not to do that again,' followed by laughter and a sense of accomplishment.

"People began to excel and show what they could do. The subsidiary turned positive almost over night. We became a family. Why? Hope was returned to people who had no hope. Pride returned to getting the job done. Excitement returned with each small success, which we all shared. The focus moved away from the failures and forward to the wins. Hope is nurtured by leadership, communication and attitude."

Charles' account contains crucial elements showing how hope helps in a crisis. To name a few, there's the upbeat attitude, the personal approach, the focus on learning, the apportioning of tasks, the celebration of success, the sense of being in it together, the bonhomie, and more. It's implicit that Salyer and his team *believed* in what they were doing.

REALITY

Credible, true hope, the kind capable of producing energy and belief, is reality based. The data we marshal to do our forecasting about the positive future we desire is the critical grounding that separates true hope from false hope, and hope from optimism. From a physician's point of view, "Hope, unlike optimism, is rooted in unalloyed reality... [acknowledging] the deep obstacles and significant pitfalls along the path. True hope has no room for delusion."[10] Reality is a distinguishing feature of hope.

When talking about the meanings of hope, John Hope Franklin, historian, activist, grandson of a slave who fought for the Union, and winner of the Presidential Medal of Freedom and more than 100 honorary degrees, referred to the Civil Rights Movement, his own life history, and indeed the "bright outlook" implied in his middle name, as sources of hope. Now 90, he has always had "himself and his self-respect... that was how I made my way." What is striking and most pertinent is that Professor Franklin's aim from the beginning has been to "rise above sentimentality," to destroy the "myths that pass as history," and to tell the truth. Hope lies in his "ability to look beyond" the current situation and see a time when things would be changed for the better.[11] Hope sticks with the truth, however difficult or cruel, and chooses, in Harold Oliver's phrase, "the reality of futurity."[12]

An orientation to reality, then, requires a dual focus and a single mode: looking beyond the present situation while keeping sight of the here-and-now, and sticking to the truth. In order to illustrate how this works in organizations, we offer the following:

- Margaret Buchanan, publisher of *The Cincinnati Enquirer* agrees that truth and truth-telling are central to reality, even though "it's harder today to keep hope alive because black and white money issues get in the way of hope and always have—the cruel realities of the bottom line."

- Executive coach and former sales director Barbara Cavalier connects hope with "truth and reality" and notices what happens in company settings:

  "When personal truth can be told, organizational truth will be known. I'm filled with hope when there's truth in the room—it's a release, a fresh start."

- Another manager made the following statement with which almost everyone would agree: "It's the hardest thing to tell the truth in business."

- John Wurzburger, a general manager at Avery Dennison, faced with the need to reduce nonvalue-adding costs, told his organization that "if we don't do what we need to do, someone else will do it for us, and we'll lose control." His unprompted view of the results of his straight talk: "I think the organization has a fair amount of hope in it right now."

- One manager told us about going in to turn around the operations of a bankrupt leasing company and yet doing it in a hopeful way:

> "We laid the facts on the table. It was not pretty. We told people we would be going from a workforce of 400 to 90 over the next two years. We laid out our strategy. We said we would post every position. We gave people the tools and knowledge to self-select their course of action."

We know well enough that "reality" can be cruel and that it's hard to tell the truth. We know too that in framing reality as having a future beyond today opens up choices and engenders hope. As a manager told us: "When we know the truth we can think about options. Options give people hope and possibilities, although at first they may have felt diminished."

Dr. Jim Votruba, president of Northern Kentucky University, spoke to us about how, in order for these themes to come together, a leader must be willing to confront reality and be vulnerable in the process. He quoted from one of his favorite leadership role models, Max DePree, former Chairman and CEO of Herman Miller, Inc.: "The first responsibility of a leader is to define reality. The last is to say thank you."[13]

One way Jim defines reality, publicly, is through his annual spring town meetings. Open to all, the meeting is designed for involvement. Jim uses a split screen; on one side he puts up "What We Say We Value," and on the other he displays "What We Funded." In this way, he can talk about opportunities, tradeoffs, and risks, as well as field questions regarding discrepancies between what the organization says and what it does. It's a chance for people to ask why and to develop a better understanding of the big picture. Jim's openness, honesty, and willingness to speak the truth contribute to a culture of hope.

Hope, then, is "recognition that there are both bad possibilities and good possibilities—focusing on the good," in the words of a manager; and in the words of an existential philosopher, "Hope is the willed response to a reality which appears to it as 'gracious.'"[14]

MEANING

In a study of the meaning of hope among Swedes, the researchers, using an ethnographic approach, found hope to be a process containing both internal and external dimensions, linked to meaning, being, and doing. Hope related to being releases energy that enables doing, and doing enhances the sense of self. Hope is a virtuous cycle that enhances the self as it helps achieve goals. And underlying is the experience of hope as a search for meaning.[15]

Breck Arnzen, a former employee of Digital Equipment Corporation and Peace Corps volunteer, has this reflection:

> "At DEC, we had a sense of mission that our technology was going to make life easier for people. I think it was this sense of mission and

purpose that gave me and others a sense of meaning and hope of a better place to live and work. Other than my years with the Peace Corps, DEC was the most idealistic organization I have ever experienced.

"I pause on the word 'idealistic.' Does that translate to hope? I think it does.

"When DEC's performance dropped and started acting like any other organization, it was remarkable how quickly it became a 'hopeless' organization."

Throughout our interviews we were struck with the degree to which hope and meaningfulness cohered—people want their efforts to amount to something large and lasting. The philosopher Peter Koestenbaum says,

"We live not in the past, we act in the here and now, but we live in the future, for the future. Death is of course the clearest indication that there's more going on in the world than to cater to our wishes. With all of the glory of free will, of hope, there is no hope unless we are connected to something bigger than us—you don't have to give it a name—that is more enduring than fragile life. If we aren't connected to something bigger than us, then there's no point in getting started."[16]

Jobs, Careers, and Callings

Robert Bellah and his associates made noteworthy distinctions among three forms of orientation toward work: the "job" to earn money, the "career" to advance in an occupation, and the "calling" to be linked with fellow workers as well as the larger community.[17] Work-as-calling is work for fulfillment and meaning. Listen to this manager on the cusp between career and calling:

"I'm getting to the end of my career here. I'm at the last point to be able to influence. I feel an urgency to make change."

And here is one who is very clear in wanting work to be somehow "more":

"I want to feel I'm in the right place, doing work that has a purpose and feeling inspired, connected by common belief that what we're doing has so much impact beyond the physical."

Recent research suggests that there may be an even distribution of job, career, and calling orientations in the workforce. For leaders, there is another key finding that bears directly on the relationship between workforce orientation and productivity: workgroups with biases toward callings versus jobs or careers are more committed to their activities, more trusting in management, and more satisfied with each other.[18]

These findings match the tale of the three masons. The first, when asked what he was up to, said "I'm laying bricks." (This is what I'm paid to do on my job.) The second said, "I'm constructing a wall." (Building buildings—that's my career.) The third said, "I'm building a cathedral." (My calling concerns higher purposes.) The connection between making meaning and performing work invites questions about the role of hope.

So what is the role of hope in making meaning both at work, and in work? The distinction between at-work and in-work is useful.[19] At-work meaningfulness speaks to issues of an organization's vision, mission and culture. Where are we headed together, and am I on board? In-work meaningfulness suggests intrinsic significance to the work itself. How well do I match up with the requirements of the job, and do I have any opportunities to "craft" the tasks to suit my strengths? Hope can stand as a point of convergence. Listen to this respondent:

> "This job—personally a big infusion of hope—is making a difference here on a scale I never thought. I'm able to help shape instead of being shaped. Our team has become a symbol of hope in the company, and it's so gratifying it keeps me coming back every day."

Hopeful organizational cultures make meaning *in* and *at* work by making connections among what I do, who I am, who we are together, and what we all do. And hopeful organizations are inclusive of individual strengths and preferences. Mike Allen, a senior executive at Banta, makes this connection persuasively: "When an organization lacks diversity, whether it be in skin color, gender, or in the diversity of ideas, it runs the risk of valuing conformity over innovation—which ultimately leads to the loss of hope."

Context and Perspective

Although we use the language of hope every day and often without much thought, we discovered in our interviews that we're usually just one probing question away from consequential issues stretching beyond the here-and-now. As a manager explained, "Hope is a long-term thing, a long-term commitment, a longer relationship with something out in front." When there is personal and organizational commitment to something "out in front," a roadmap is needed, a context and a sense of perspective.

Listening to people talk about their experience of hope at work, we heard a comingling of past, present, and future: past experience and present reality providing grounding for future aspirations. William Lynch, S.J., suggested in his early and influential psychological treatise that through imagination hope helps us live "outside the prison of the instant." Living in context makes hope "steadier and more mature."[20] Contextualizing hope validates peoples' past experience and wisdom, their present reality and their faith in the future. In the words of British management theorist Charles Handy:

> "We need to have faith in the future to believe in the present . . . one of the most important tasks of leadership is to point to some kind of continuity, both forward and backward. Without that sense of continuity there is no point in sacrificing any of the present for the future."[21]

In our experience catalyzing hope is often a matter of putting things in context. We've learned that organizational memory is crucial to organizational future—that a group can look forward with confidence only about as far as it can look back. Drawing out the experience of the working community is a key element in summoning and sustaining hope, just as Dr. Groopman says it works for individuals: "Hope integrates information and feelings derived from present circumstances, and it also draws on experiences of the past, seeking models and direction . . . ."[22]

Here is an example where a leader uses a timeline exercise to put the present in context and clears the way for the future. Shirley Bunger has been with Hewlett-Packard for eight years. In her current role as Director of Brand Innovation, she, along with the company, has been through some challenging times. In that context, Shirley sees her team as a "beacon of light, something different, liberating," which makes *how* they do their work as important as *what* they do:

> "I'm really conscious about coming to everything with a positive attitude. I never want my team to be a source of whining around the water cooler. I call it when things aren't working, but frame it in a positive way, not being either a negative force or a Pollyanna."

Shirley created a timeline that included 250 people from HP's marketing community. CEO, Carly Fiorina, had just left the company, and the head of marketing resigned shortly thereafter.

> "We needed to reconnect as a community. On the first day of a two-day meeting we talked about change, and on the second day, we built a timeline 60 feet long. We looked at over 65 years of HP history—milestones, accomplishments—'this is HP.' We used oral history—so much wonderful stuff. People talked about their first experience with HP. I thought I was going to cry. People were so responsive—'thank you for reminding me' or 'I never knew.' That exercise pulled me through and united people in a positive way.
>
> "One of the best ways I know to keep hope alive is to go back to some solid point I can work from—find some solid ground and

some common ground. Politics, budget, turmoil, all those things can be so divisive and cause people to lose sight of the big picture which connects us all. But you can look at that wall and you can see what a small piece this year is—1/65th of that history—and that helps put things in perspective. We've weathered change before."

As Shirley's timeline exercise reminded people how they were meaningfully connected, it bolstered their resilience in an uncertain time. The science writer, Daniel Goleman, gives evidence that "from the perspective of emotional intelligence, having hope means that one will not give in to over-whelming anxiety, a defeatist attitude, or depression in the face of difficult challenges or setbacks."[23]

Hope becomes "steadier and more mature" to the extent a community is able to see the whole continuum of past, present, and future. In the words of one leader, "The organization can 'laugh' at tough times knowing they are blips with the trend eventually going forward." And another:

"The work is seen more as the long term. A marathon is not a sprint. Winning means a season, not just a game."

Context, perspective—and resilience: gifts of hope.

> *The very least you can do in your life is to figure out what you hope for. And the most you can do is live inside that hope. Not admire it from a distance but live right in it, under its roof.*
>
> *Barbara Kingsolver*

HEADS, HEARTS, HANDS ... AND FEET

We define hope as an orientation toward a positive future that engages our heads, hearts and hands. One of our respondents would add feet:

"Many years ago when I first started working in the consulting world, I had one of those seminal conversations with an older man, a top execu-tive at Dow Brands. We were working on designing a training univer-sity—we had done all the right things: learning objectives, career paths, a great curriculum and course catalogue, revamped evaluation system, rewards and recognition, etc. When we had everything pretty much set (I thought), he said: 'OK, now we need to put it in shoes.'

"What he meant was: We need to make this real. What does it look like 'walking around in shoes?' How does this become part of the daily life of this organization? *For me, Hope is always wearing shoes.* It's not something purely spiritual or emotional. On some days, hope is more of an idea and less of a part of my being—and maybe all I can do is literally put one foot in front of the other. On other days, I have 'diamonds on the soles of my shoes.'"

This image captures the experience of hope at work: sometimes having "no reason," never "purely emotional or spiritual," always grounded and moving forward.

Chapter 3

Hope's Rewards

People flourish when they feel hope in their neighborhood and in their bones.[1]
Lionel Tiger

From research in many fields, we are beginning to learn more about what hope is and how hope works, an important first step in redressing the asymmetry of dark versus light in our time. As Martin E.P. Seligman writes in the first sentence of *Authentic Happiness,* his call-to-arms for positive psychology, "for the past half century psychology has been consumed with a single topic only—mental illness...."[2] Here we document the sea change that is taking place in leadership and organizational research.

A recent, comprehensive survey of social science research over the past forty years has reached the conclusion that there is a "disappointingly relentless pattern," which is that "bad is stronger than good, as a general principle across a broad range of psychological phenomena." The list of scientific findings is as impressive as it is depressing: bad feedback, bad parenting, bad events of any kind, and even having a bad day all produce more emotions and have more lasting effects than good. There are more words for bad emotions than good. Punishment is stronger than reward. The person we hope never to be is a more powerful motivator than the person we aspire to be. There's much more.[3]

Why is this so and what is the role of hope? The researchers suggest that from the standpoint of survival, it is adaptive for bad to be stronger than good. When we're attuned to danger, we're more likely to avoid it. When a possible good is missed, we may feel regret; when a bad outcome is ignored, it can be very costly indeed. Research into advertising campaigns for medicines conducted in fifteen American cities compared positive appeals with a strongly negative one—the positive appeals caused sales to decline by 10% while the negative appeals grew sales by 171%.[4] Yet when a negative orientation takes over completely, as it can in organizations as well as individual lives, there is likely to be defeat, despair, and even demise. Emotional appeals that are negative serve to narrow perceptions, and as a result there is a loss of creativity, risk-taking, enthusiasm—and hope.

The role of hope, in our view, is to outmaneuver rather than outnumber the bad. When we hope, we put ourselves on a path toward a preferred future, with good at our side, and leave the bad behind. Like sunflowers, we are inclined to turn our faces toward the light. In the words of Dr. Fred Loya, a psychologist and Executive Director of Santa Anita Family Services, "All of us move in the direction of the light of hope." In this chapter, we highlight hope's rewards for individuals, teams, and organizations and show how hope ditches darkness.

> *Hope is a word we have known from the beginning. Even before the word, hope has been with us as an instinct, a feeling, an impulse, a thought. We know it so well, yet we forget what an important role it plays in every aspect of our being.*
>
> *Alice Rose George and Lee Marks*

INDIVIDUAL REWARDS

In the last three decades social scientists have attempted to measure hope objectively and "convert it to a number" so it could be correlated with any number of factors, situations, and outcomes. In a recent handbook of positive psychological assessment it is reported that there are at least twenty-six definitions of hope in use and so many scales and measures that there is "confusion and ambiguity."[5] A recent review of hope as a variable by Jaklin Eliott notes the complexity of the task and concludes more research is needed. Eliott notes, however, that everyone who measures hope is in implicit agreement that it is individual, objective, variable, and worthwhile.[6] For our purposes, the results of such studies—assuming that what is being measured by hope scales is at least an authentic expression of hope—can indicate the breadth of rewards that hope has for the individual.

C. Rick Snyder and his team of colleagues in the Hope Research Group at the University of Kansas have been developing and refining their "hope theory" since 1991, when they defined hope as "a positive motivational state that is based on an interactively derived sense of successful (1) agency (goal-directed energy), and (2) pathways (planning to meet goals)."[7] In their current view, there is a third factor to consider, the goals themselves—they need to be important and adaptive. These three components are "positive, reciprocal and iterative," and they yield multiple beneficial outcomes.[8]

Within hope theory, there is considerable specificity as to what hope is, and Snyder is very clear about what hope is not:

Not Pollyanna Optimism (being naive and lacking compassion)

Not Learned Optimism (distancing oneself from failure)

Not Type A Behavior Pattern (being impatient and uncompromising)

Nasruddin was riding the train to work as he does every day and the conductor asked him for his ticket. He reached into his coat pocket, and finding nothing rifled through his pants pocket and then his briefcase. Still not finding it, he looked on the floor in the aisle and under his seat. His panic growing, Nasruddin began to ask the other passengers if they had seen or could help him look.

Finally the conductor asked: "Why don't you look in your shirt pocket? That's where most people keep their tickets."

"I couldn't do that," he said, "because if I looked there and the ticket wasn't there, I'd be without any hope."

Attributed to Coleman Barks

Not Emotion and Self-Esteem (failing to be thoughtful or to achieve)

Not Intelligence or Previous Achievement (—hope can be learned)

Not Useless (—hope is broadly beneficial)

Not Vague (—the Hope Scale is quite specific).[9]

Snyder's Hope Scale has been proven to have excellent psychometric qualities and has been employed in diverse ways to understand the psychological assets that accrue to 'high-hope' people. Here is a brief summary from two recent reports:[10]

- *Hope helps academic performance:* Hope predicts grades and graduation rates among college students and correlates with teacher encouragement.
- *Hope increases athletic performance:* High-hope athletes outperform their lower-hope counterparts even when athletic ability is accounted for, and athletes who are trained in hopeful thinking increase their self-confidence.
- *Hope contributes to physical health:* People with higher hopes may have greater knowledge about illnesses and more willingness to act on that knowledge, including engaging in exercise, and they may also cope better with pain and disability.
- *Hope contributes to psychological health:* Higher hope is correlated with positive thinking and feelings of self-worth, and with the ability to call on family and friends in times of need.
- *Hope assists in the achievement of goals:* Higher-hope people typically employ flexibility in their thinking so they are less likely to become stuck.
- *Hope encourages connection:* Higher hope people have more satisfaction related to interpersonal interactions—and greater meaning in their lives.

Snyder reports that the strongest correlation of the Hope Scale is with self-actualization[11]—Maslow's construct that the human being has within

> "... a pressure toward full individuality and identity, toward seeing the truth rather than being blind, toward being creative, toward being good, and a lot else. That is, the human being is so constructed that he presses toward fuller and fuller being and this means toward what most people would call good values, toward serenity, kindness, courage, honesty, love, unselfishness, and goodness."[12]

In general, hopeful people perform at the highest levels and in a word, are winners.

Dr. Jerome Groopman, M.D., a physician at Harvard Medical School and chief of experimental medicine at Beth Deaconess Medical Center in Boston who is also a respected science writer, has recently explored the role of hope in health and healing. "As a scientist" and from his own experience with cancer patients he has come to believe that "there is an authentic biology of hope." According to Dr. Groopman, belief and expectation are key elements of hope, releasing endorphins and enkephalins in the brain that act to block pain, and unleashing a "domino effect, a chain reaction in which each link makes improvement more likely. It changes us profoundly in spirit and body."[13]

Groopman interviewed Dr. Richard Davidson at the University of Wisconsin, an expert on the biology of positive emotions, and learned about another of hope's rewards—"affective forecasting," the good feelings you experience when you anticipate a positive future. The brain takes you out of your current state and shifts your mood upward, out of the reach of the "bad." Hope therefore "has wings," Groopman concludes.[14] The allusion is to Emily Dickinson's famous line that "Hope is the thing with feathers."

The story William Buchholz, M.D. told in a medical journal about hope's efficacy is worth retelling here:

> "As I was eating breakfast one morning I overheard two oncologists discussing the papers they were to present that day at the national meeting of the American Society of Clinical Oncology. One was complaining bitterly."

> "You know, Bob, I just don't understand it. We used the same drugs, the same dosage, the same schedule, and the same entry criteria. Yet I got a 22% response rate and you got 74%. That's unheard of for metastatic lung cancer. How do you do it?"

> "We're both using Etoposide, Platinol, Oncovin, and Hydroxyurea. You call yours EPOH. I tell my patients I'm giving them HOPE.

Sure, I tell them this is experimental, and we go over the long list of side effects together. But I emphasize that we have a chance. As dismal as the statistics are for non-small cell, there are always a few percent who do really well."

"Aren't you giving them false hope with that approach? What do you do if they don't respond?"

"Alan,...don't you give them false despair when you stress only the side effects of the treatment and the grimness of the prognosis? It's not ethical to minimize those. Neither is it fair to shut out the possibility of a good outcome. When patients have hope, they are motivated, they withstand the chemotherapy better. When they look to the future, they may be afraid, but at least they have something to hold on to."

"Realistically, most will not survive the disease. I never promise cure. What I can offer, however, is my pledge not to abandon them. I can help patients switch their goals from cure to remission, from remission to control, and finally, from control to death that is comfortable and as meaningful as possible."

"My breakfast was over, and as I got up to leave, I thought, maybe I'll give my patients a little hope next time, too!"[15]

And so on an individual basis, the doctors and social researchers are telling us, hope works. We talked with many hopeful people who would no doubt earn high scores on a hope scale or a physiological test. Listen to how they described hope—and themselves:

"Hope is very strong. It gives you passion and enthusiasm, makes you want to do more."

"I love what I'm doing."

"It's a feeling of being filled up, fully alive."

"It's a higher level of energy and motivation."

"Having hope is a solid bundle in my gut."

"I can be accepted as a person with an idea regardless of my function."

"When things are not great, I keep my perspective."

"Hope carries us forward to make a difference on the planet."

"Hope gives you courage."

"Hope is more fun. Life is too short for negative energy."

"I'm filled up, feeling fully alive, and looking forward to, even energized about, what's next."

"I know I feel hope, when I spring out of bed in the morning, when
I sing in the shower, when I think good things can happen, and
when I have a positive vision of where I am going and what I can
accomplish."

And as for putting hope to work: "When I feel hope at work I am inspired to
achieve something greater."

TEAM REWARDS

Despite the increasing body of proof that hope has rewards for the individual, "To date, hope has had little application to the workplace or the
leadership field."[16] The study of hope in teams and organizations is in its
infancy. Yet work is under way. Preliminary studies, though narrow in scope,
are intriguing. For example, in a recent survey, the hope of workers in a
Chinese company was positively related to their performance.[17] And in the
first empirical study of the relationship between the hope of a leader, financial
performance, and employee satisfaction—in a chain of fast-food franchises in
the Midwest—higher-hope leaders outperformed their peers. At statistically
significant levels, their work units had higher profits and more satisfied
employees with lower turnover.[18]

In the first use of a hope scale in occupational psychology, using a sample
of 450 nurses in two hospitals, hope had a significant positive relationship
with perceptions of health. Further, it was found that ICU nurses, half of the
study, whose work contains the greatest exposure to death and dying,
reported higher hope and health than their colleagues in other roles.
These findings suggest that the ability to be fully engaged on the job, no
matter the demands of the workload, enhances satisfaction and pleasure, and
reduces barriers to hope. What is the strongest negative correlation with
hope? Role ambiguity—not knowing what is expected or what to do
about it.[19] Hopeful work is clear about responsibilities and well supported
with tools and training.

Wendy Wilson-Bett is Global Capabilities Director for Cadbury
Schweppes. In her twenty years with the company she has had both marketing and general management roles, so following a reorganization a couple of
years ago, in which many people changed roles, she anxiously awaited her
new assignment. "A lot of the roles my new boss, the new President of Global
Commercial, Nick Fell, had to offer were hard-edged, with clear bottom line
accountability, so when I was offered the role of developing a new capability
program for the commercial area, I was a little concerned that it wasn't a big
enough challenge or the right next step in my career." When Wendy talked to

her manager about it, however, he convinced her of two things: that her job was critical to driving growth, and that she could make a difference to the future of the whole company.

He did many things to fuel Wendy's hope:

"He allowed me to dream, allowed me to believe I could make changes, and backed it up not only with money but with his time. He participated in every key development meeting and key training event. He has walked the talk from the very start. It would have been so easy to go for incrementalism, but he set the bar high, expected great things and then laughed when I said I wanted to set it even higher, in order to beat his expectations! Because the ambitious goal we set ourselves in the end was not imposed, I always believed it was doable."

Now, several years later, on the back of the highly successful development of the capability program, active support from other leaders in the business including the CEO, and other important changes to the business, Wendy can see signs of growing confidence and hope:

"The confidence and passion that my team have in their ability is tangible. They know they have pulled off something great. The confidence across the business is also growing as a result of a number of very positive changes in the company. Now you hear people talking—heads held higher than they used to be, about beating the competition. They have more self-confidence, less self-doubt. You can feel the optimism.

"Rather than negative words, excuses and alibis, people are speaking more passionately about opportunity, growth and innovation. Confidence to speak one's mind is starting to build. It's reversing the old negative cycle of corridor conversations, where people would talk privately about their real views, but publicly, in meetings, they would feel obliged to agree with the most senior leader.

"I believe it's the hardest thing in business to tell the whole truth, to tell it as it is, especially when you know it's something other people don't agree with or don't want to hear. But if we can actively encourage it, it's the fastest way to great feedback and learning, and the smartest way to get great ideas which work.

"By fostering these new behaviors and reinforcing the idea that no single person has all the answers, we are gradually building people's confidence that it's fine to have a different opinion, as long as it's validated by sound reasoning. Of course, this really relies on trust, and that's something you have to earn from each other. With the levels of enthusiasm I have seen for the changes here and the continued strong and passionate leadership from the top, I really believe the change will make a difference to our company's future—the very thing Nick inspired me to dream about 2 years ago."

As hope in the workplace becomes a mainstream topic, and as we continue to understand more about the vital role it plays in our mental and physical well-being, leaders are invited to consider what a growing number of organizational scholars and practitioners are saying, namely "to nurture organizational conditions that unleash human hope may well be our most important task."[21]

ORGANIZATIONAL REWARDS

In the area of organizational behavior, the emerging field of *Positive Organizational Scholarship* (POS) "focuses on dynamics such as excellence, thriving, flourishing, abundance, resilience and virtuousness." POS distinguishes itself from traditional organizational studies in that it "seeks to understand what represents the best of the human condition."[22] As two proponents explain: "The argument is that as people throughout the organization become increasingly aware of the positive core, appreciation escalates, hope grows, and the community expands."[23] Here are four examples to illustrate how the rewards of hope can be spread across entire institutions and companies.

First, Ian Mitroff, a professor at the University of Southern California and his colleague, Elizabeth Denton performed a "spiritual audit" of U.S. corporations and described five organizational forms that possess "a fundamental, underlying *principle of hope*."[24] Here is how hope works in each: In a religion-based organization, such as Huntsman Chemical in Utah, hope is deeply connected to belief in God. In an evolutionary organization, where Tom's of Maine is an example, hope is held in the proposition that environmentalism will yield profit, and vice versa. Alcoholics Anonymous is a recovering organization where working the program is the act of hope. A socially responsible organization, such as Ben & Jerry's, expresses hope through its commitment to social ethics. Finally, a values-based organization, such as Kingston Technology in California, derives hope from explicit adherence to universal values such as the Golden Rule. According to Mitroff and Denton, the data suggest that spiritual organizations such as these succeed ahead of their less spiritual counterparts—associates feel less fearful, more authentic, and better engaged, and they perceive their organizations as being more successful.

Second, Donald Berwick, MD, founder and CEO of the Institute for Healthcare Improvement and a recent recipient of an honorary knighthood for contributions to Britain's National Health Service, spoke in a recent interview about how to improve healthcare. He downplayed external motivational schemes such as pay-for-performance as well as structural changes in the system and emphasized the positive force of intrinsic motivation—organizational energy that can be tapped through hope:

"The reservoir—the latent will in the workforce to do better—is absolutely overwhelming. It's like drilling for oil. There is so much pent-up need in the healthcare workforce—and I include here not just doctors, but nurses, pharmacists, respiratory therapists, managers—to really do better. It's so easy to get there once you decide to. It's a constant source of energy to find that people want to be better at what they do. Once you give them an authentic invitation to do that, it's so much fun and so inspiring."[25]

Third, in 2001, *Success* Magazine commissioned a survey of hopefulness in U.S. companies and received useful data on 125 firms ranging in size from 8 to 40,000 associates. The ten most hopeful companies were analyzed to determine commonalities—all ten were prospering—and this is what was found:

1. CEOs who "work hard to create trust respect, and genuine affection."
2. Concrete goals: "all employees are aware of what must be done" and they seek "good and multiple routes to desired goals."
3. Managers who show "respect and care about employee job performance, *as well as their personal lives.*"
4. Strong communications and "an environment in which independent thought and discourse are encouraged."
5. Cultures that rest on a "level playing field" and that value innovation, risk and integrity.

Thus hope is reflected in organizational development and social change approaches that value dialogue, gratitude and appreciation, action-learning, work redesign, and civic virtue. The study concluded: "These are workplaces of growth and happiness that are built on foundations of hope."[26]

And fourth, The Corporate Leadership Council, an executive network for leaders of the world's organizations, public and private, surveyed more than 50,000 employees in more than fifty-nine organizations around the world and learned how much "employee engagement" means to performance. The extent to which workers commit to something or someone in their organizations matters significantly—increased commitment can mean an 87% increase in employees' willingness to continue on the payroll, a 57% enhancement in employees' willingness to go the extra mile, and a 20% improvement in results. Engagement was analyzed as being a function of two kinds of commitment: *rational commitment* (when my job serves my financial, developmental, or professional self-interest), and *emotional commitment* (when I value, enjoy, and believe in what I do). From the perspective of hope, the coincident finding is that emotional commitment had *four times* the power of rational commitment to affect performance.[27]

Emotional commitment gives people the courage and self-confidence to speak truth to power—to propose ideas that are new or that challenge conventional wisdom and paradigms. Listen to how one person described her experience at two companies—the first drained her of hope while the second opened her capacity for passion and courage:

> "I was 15 pounds heavier, exhausted, and mentally drained. I had no energy when I got home to play with the kids. As I saw outside companies and people interested in me, hope started coming back.

> "I left and joined a new company and again I felt appreciated. I went from being constantly questioned to being really listened to and impacting the business. I felt smart and capable and valued again. I love knowing there's a promise of creating. It's so much fun. You see opportunities to contribute—that's empowering.

> "Hope means not being shot down. When I am accepted as a person with an idea, regardless of my function, my level of confidence is so much higher. I can go in and be respected and say and speak up and retain my stature. I now love what I'm doing."

Hope builds courage, which bolsters self-confidence, which creates more courage and hope in a virtuous cycle. The end result is, in the words of a manager, both "empowering and energizing, a feeling of being supported, not going it alone," and in the words of another, "a solid bundle in my gut." Nurturing hope in organizations may look as small as "seeing my ideas informing decisions," but the rewards are great in terms of overall engagement.

Hope is an approach to employee happiness and health—not just a means to higher productivity. Hope's goals are therefore ends in themselves, and a hopeful organization understands the value of intrinsic worth, as this leader knows:

> "Hope is present in an organization when you can see it on the faces of the staff, feel it in their attitude towards what they do each day, and by the laughter that echoes through the halls. A group that has hope faces each new day with a 'we can do it' attitude. The interaction is positive and upbeat. Projects are attacked with the concept of when it will be done not how or if it will be done. People are smiling, jovial, almost giddy at times. They want to succeed. They want to participate.

They look for answers and ways to solve problems versus studying the issues for the downside and potential failure quotient."

Hope in itself is not a strategy, nor is it enough to ensure organizational success. "Hope is not the answer," we were told, "but it can sustain you until find the answer." When hope is present in organizations, people think, feel, and act differently; they exhibit courage, and they develop and use capabilities that contribute to engagement, to results, and to a sense of well-being.

Chapter 4

Hope's Companions and Competitors

Hope is *"goodness in a tight spot, and ambitious to prove things."*[1]

Lance Morrow

Before diving deep into hope's principles, let's step back and make some distinctions to clarify what hope is and isn't. We think of hope's companions and competitors. The companions—wishful thinking, prayer, and optimism—are naturally related to hope in positive ways. The competitors— pessimism, fear, and denial—while apparently at odds with hope, can play important and sometimes constructive roles. We will also speak briefly about evil, a true adversary. Our intention is to clear the way for hope as a true ally of leadership.

HOPE'S COMPANIONS

An underlying issue concerns the phrase "realistic hope" and its companion "false hope." Who determines whether hope is realistic? When do you know hope is realistic? And what are the consequences if hope is proven unrealistic?

Experts in any field, be it medicine, education, or business, are prone to lead with their expertise in a given matter and get "all the facts out on the table" in order to serve rational decision making and preserve individual autonomy. Thus, a medical doctor may feel compelled to convey the "realities" of a poor prognosis to a patient, a guidance counselor may dampen the enthusiasm of an "average" student making application to a competitive college, and a supervisor may want to give an underperforming subordinate some "direct feedback." Perhaps each receiver of information in these three cases is hopeful of a positive outcome: the patient is hopeful for recovery, the student is hopeful for admission to a college of choice, and the employee for a salary raise. Who decides if hope is unrealistic? Is it the hoper, or the person in charge?

In each case, there are conceivably two sets of hopes, and both sets may indeed be realistic. Doctor and patient, guidance counselor and student, supervisor and employee may be holding *different* hopes, hopes not necessarily in conflict. Can we say one hope is more realistic than another? Is it the place of the expert or authority figure, therefore, to "impose" or "depose" a hope? And the fact is that we often don't know whether hopes are realistic until after the fact. If a hoper "defeats the odds" and gets healthy, gets admitted to a top school, or becomes a superior performer, is this not an argument *for* "unrealistic" hope?

The point is that having an expansive view of a situation is highly adaptive. Hope takes reality as "what is *and* what could be," refusing to be content with "just what is." Hope's illusions, therefore, are starting positions in a journey of trial-and-error—not immutable errors in judgment. (To keep things straight, illusions are *not delusions*, which are debilitating distortions that don't respond to reality; illusions can change.) When illusions are positive, they spur people to take charge and get things done. This is the essence of leadership charisma, after all. When we are inspired by leaders—rather than completely enthralled—we are given to believe that we can do more and do it better than we might believe on our own.

People with high hope, according to research, distort reality in such a way that they feel confident, they set more goals and higher goals, and they exercise creativity. As a result, high-hopers increase the likelihood of their success.[2] So, within a reasonable range, positive illusions are facilitative, not false.

Wishful Thinking

Wishful thinking has gotten a bad name. A manager told us, "Sometimes hope seems more wishing for, than doing," the implication being that wishing is a passive and ineffective activity. Colloquially, "wishy-washy" means lacking in strength of character or purpose. The old Scottish proverb, "If wishes were horses, beggars would ride," suggests wishing comes easily but amounts to little.

In our view, wishing is a creative act of imagination that sets the stage for hope. It's a good thing to wish, especially at work, and to wish expansively and publicly. According to Freud, "nothing but a wish can set our mental apparatus to work."[3] Asking members of a work team to reveal their wishes for their company or unit, for example, to say how they'd like to serve their customers, what they'd like to change or create, or how they'd prefer to interact with each other, can unleash new thinking and energy. Of course

HOPE's Companions

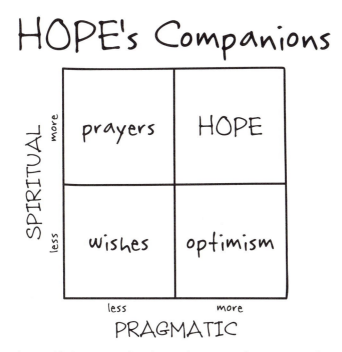

wishing by itself doesn't make things happen. The point is that wishing deserves more respect, and it can lead the way to hope.

The following chart locates wishing in relation to two other companions of hope. Note that wishing is a valuable precursor though naturally low in spiritual force and pragmatic effect.

Prayer

Our use of the word spiritual is not very precise and not meant to be. The language of spirituality is problematic—it connotes many things to many people. For us, spirituality includes states of mindfulness, feelings of transcendence, occurrences of flow, practices of meditation, disciplines of consciousness, and of course prayers. We understand spirituality as an inner experience of humanness and a place where hope resides.

So by our definition prayer is spiritual, but is it pragmatic? Can prayers heal? Evidence is inconclusive, and though many scientists are open minded, many remain skeptical.[4]

Herbert Benson, Harvard Medical School cardiologist and pioneering founder of the Mind/Body Medical Institute, is not one of the skeptics. The "relaxation response" elicited by such behaviors as prayer, meditation, yoga, tai chi, and repetitive exercise, he points out, is connected to release of nitric oxide in the body, the substance that counteracts the damaging effects of the stress hormone norepinephrine. "Hope in something beyond the illness...gives purpose to life," according to Benson, and helps the body heal.[5]

Harold Koenig, a professor of psychiatry and medicine at Duke University who is the director and founder of the Center for the Study of Religious/ Spirituality and Health at Duke, suggests that "religion not only adds years to life, but life to years." Further, he believes in the medical power of prayer. "The religious belief system is a very optimistic, very hopeful, very meaningful world view that gives each person an important and essential place in the universe...."[6]

Yet recently, 544 brain researchers signed a petition to cancel a lecture by the Dalai Lama at the annual meeting of the Society for Neuroscience. Why? There are disputes about whether practices of meditation and mindfulness promote compassion, happiness, or other welcome outcomes. Some scientists are saying there is no proof; others point out that brain scans during meditation show increased levels of neural activity in regions of the brain associated with positive emotion. Dr. Robert Wyman, a neurobiologist at Yale, said, "This research is a first pass on a new topic, and you can't do perfect science the first time through."[7] So even more than with hope, research is under way to learn about the nature and positive effects of prayer and meditation.

Optimism

Although hope and optimism are often thrown in together and treated as interchangeable parts, there are important differences. The environmentalist Mark Hertsgaard defines optimism as "the belief that things will turn out well," as compared to hope: "an active, determined conviction that is rooted in the spirit, chosen by the heart, and guided by the mind."[8]

Optimism has its strengths, and in the realm of psychological research an "optimism bandwagon" has been forming, according to Christopher Peterson, so much so that he has words of caution.[9] Too much optimism gets us to the Pollyanna-ish view of the world, so single-minded we *always* look at the bright side of things. We're reminded of the quip, often repeated in corporate settings, that if you're not confused in the face of complexity, you obviously don't know what's going on. Thus, relentless, irrepressible optimism in a leader turns people off and invites cynicism.

Martin E.P. Seligman, whose research on optimism is helping change psychology, now prefers to speak of "warranted optimism."[10] For example, it has been found that optimism doesn't function like denial—optimists attend to relevant risks and tend to be realistic when information is negative.[11] Yet indeed, compared to pessimists and realists, optimists are better able to manage anxiety, which aids in decision making and getting a move on.[12]

The research on illusions is closely connected to what is known about optimism. Call it the Lake Wobegone effect, where according to the story-teller Garrison Keillor, "all the women are strong, the men are good-looking, and the children are above average." It happens that most people see themselves as both better than the average person and better than how other people see them. Also, people generally have unjustified beliefs in their personal control and will act as if they have control in situations where they really don't. Furthermore, most people prefer the present to the past, and prefer the future to the present. These "positive illusions" are actually adaptive—illusions promote happiness, the ability to care for others, and the capacity for productive work. "The mentally healthy person appears to have the enviable capacity to distort reality in a direction that enhances self-esteem, maintains beliefs in personal efficacy, and promotes an optimistic view of the future."[13] As we see it, optimism, best taken in moderation, is one of hope's closest colleagues.

Hope is definitely not the same thing as optimism. It is not the conviction that something will turn out well, but the certainty that something makes sense, regardless of how it turns out.

Vaclav Havel

What optimism lacks is hope's sense of the spiritual and its more pragmatic engagement. In the words of the professor of religion, Cornel West, "Optimism adopts the stance of the spectator who surveys the evidence in order to infer that things are going to get better," while "Hope enacts the stance of the participant who actively struggles against the evidence...."[14] Said differently, hope draws its power from within in order to reach positive goals, whereas optimism expects something good to happen while taking pains to segregate itself from the negative.[15]

One of our respondents wondered about these things in the following way:

"Maybe hope is faith in its best suit. It's no good if it is a cover for what is really true about some circumstance. But if it's a tap into the beyond, to the place where we KNOW who we are and where we should be, then it is a powerful instrument of focus in the worst of times."

And a manager in marketing research, made this distinction for us:

"I'm sure you've thought of the differences between optimism and hope, but I would distinguish these concepts along the lines of William James' discussion (in the *Varieties of Religious Experience*) of 'once-born' and 'twice-born' souls. The former are optimistic by temperament, never having suffered a crisis of faith, etc. The latter (including James himself) have struggled to achieve something that looks like optimism but is somehow deeper because of this experience. I think that's more what you have in mind by hope?"

Indeed it is. For leaders and their organizations, the lessons of hope's companions are: Unleash the imagination and creativity inherent in wishful thinking, enhance mind-body connections for everyone in the workforce by acknowledging the importance of the human spirit in daily work, and establish an optimistic culture that expects no less than success. Hope makes friends with these companions because of its mysterious ability to make a difference.

HOPE'S COMPETITORS

This section is as brief as the topics are vast. Again, our intent is to describe how hope coexists with seeming opposites.

Pessimism

In some of our interviews, we heard strong words of workplace pessimism that went well beyond normal grousing to border on despair:

"They're raising the bar so high it's unachievable."

"We lost eight managers out of nine in less than two years. There's no hope for the future, no light at the end of the tunnel."

"Because of the constant reorganization, uncertainty, not knowing, and not being focused, you can't hear. Your only hope is that maybe you'll have a job."

"To deliver the bare minimum, you have to work eleven-hour days, with insufficient resources, and even when you deliver it's not enough."

It would be easy to conclude that these expressions are sure signs of workplace dysfunction—they certainly sounded that way to us. Wrapped up in these feelings we sensed energetic frustration emanating from a belief that things should and indeed could be better. The speakers might not have been predicting happy outcomes for themselves or their companies, yet if they were to make themselves truly heard in their organizations, and if their sentiments were effectively addressed, we would anticipate progress. For us, then, pessimism means taking a dim view of reality—but not giving in to darkness. Pessimism is the opposite of optimism, after all, only semantically. Optimism and pessimism are not really opposites in a psychological sense.[16] The respondents quoted above can be both bleak and buoyant about their jobs *at the same time.*

We hold pessimism as one of hope's competitors because it can overwhelm. Even still, it can be useful. Psychologist Julie Norem has shown that pessimism is most adaptive when it is "defensive."[17] The real enemy in her view is *anxiety*, not negativity. Anxiety hurts health and disrupts performance. "Defensive pessimists," feeling anxious about future performance, take steps to anticipate and account for whatever they feel is still in their control. The defensive pessimist is hopeful that by focusing on advance preparations without expecting success, he or she will control anxiety and therefore improve the ability to perform. Thus he or she has hope just as much as a strategic optimist, though coming at it from a different direction. By ignoring the possibility of failure and choosing not to get consumed with advance preparations, the strategic optimist will keep performance anxiety compartmentalized and therefore improve his or her ability to perform. Pessimists and optimists are really not "pure types." In the main, people are both, employing either pessimism or optimism in different situations or indeed both in a single event.

For leaders, here are three explicit recommendations stemming from defensive pessimism and strategic optimism:

First, don't maximize optimism or dismiss pessimism. Both are needed in measure, although it's better to have a surfeit of optimism.

Second, when you rehearse the negative, do it before the fact, not after. At the end of the day—no matter the outcome—debrief, take stock, capture lessons learned, celebrate or make amends, recommit to current directions or change plans, but by all means don't ruminate. Move on.

Third, consider how you can put more optimism into your company culture while keeping pessimism in some of your checks and balances.[18] Hopeful companies encourage risk and creativity, hallmarks of optimism, even as they mind the store with an appropriate measure of pessimism, attending to safety and accountability.

Fear

Philosophers have long understood fear and hope as close competitors. Here's Spinoza: "There is no hope unmingled with fear, and no fear unmingled with hope";[19] and David Hume: "When either good or evil is uncertain, it gives rise to FEAR or HOPE, according to the degrees of uncertainty on the one side or the other";[20] and La Rochefoucauld: "Hope and fear are inseparable."[21] Though we didn't ask them directly, some of our respondents were completely in tune with these ideas:

> "I didn't know I had hope because I covered it up for years because of fear—feeding fear, anger, sorrow, regret."

> "Fear comes back. Hope is the only thing that takes it away."

> "Hope is important, but so is fear. Fear has urgency. The world tends to be unbalanced towards fear."

It's a workplace myth that fear motivates positive change—fear motivates anxiety, denial, or automatic responses.[22] And it's a myth that fear, rather than joy and love, spurs creativity.[23] Yet fear has a particular edge on hope. Unlike hope, fear is an automatic emotion with a physiological basis, and "emotionality supercedes rationality in both timing and influence."[24]

Hope needs to be rational to combat fear through imagination and reason. Hope also needs to be emotional to energize purpose and stimulate action. Furthermore, hope needs to be social, enlisting others in the fray. In competitive terms, hope fights an uphill though winnable fight with fear.

A creative strategy for hope is to *reframe* fear. After all, fear can't think, it can only intimidate. Perhaps this is ultimately the task of leadership. An American President once rallied the hopeful, saying: "The only thing we have to fear is fear itself—nameless, unreasoning, unjustified terror," and he helped change the course of history. The cognitive behaviorist Stanley Rachman notes that for a number of years research in behavior therapy was focused on the nature of fear, until it came to be realized that frightened patients could be taught to face their fears. Then the research paradigm began to shift from its imbalanced focus on fear, to courage, and from focusing on courageous actors to courageous acts.[25] In so doing, fear was reframed.

Organizations live with fear, they feel fear and face fear, or they don't survive. Effective leaders know how fear and hope compete and know how to make certain that hope has the upper hand.

Nadezhda Mandelstam, a survivor of Stalin's labor camps and widow of the poet Osip Mandelstam, who didn't survive, says in her memoir that "Fear is a gleam of hope," an assertion of the will to live.[26] When we lose hope, we also lose fear, for there's nothing to be afraid of. Losing our willingness to fight, we simply accept what's coming and go quietly to meet our fate.

Denial

The problem with denial is that we don't know what we don't know and therefore fail to notice. R.D. Laing, the psychiatrist and author of the well-known verse-puzzles in *Knots*, helps us realize our predicament:

"The range of what we think and do
is limited by what we fail to notice.
And because we fail to notice
that we fail to notice, there is little we can do
to change
until we notice how failing to notice
shapes our thoughts and deeds."[27]

One of the managers we interviewed spoke of how hard it is to see things coming when you're in the middle of them. This is the "boiled frog" syndrome, not noticing when water temperature is rising, degree by degree, until it's too late to get out. Is it possible to be "too hopeful," and therefore to hang on too long? Denial prevents us from accepting "sunk costs" in financial or psychological terms—in other words, investments already down the drain with no hope of a return.

Listen to two respondents speaking about the interaction of hope and denial:

"Deming said to push out fear, because without fear, we just have what is. The whole quality and Toyota Production system movement is based on 'observation of the actual.' There is not hope in this. Only what is and how do we make that better."

"When I think of Buddhism, I am not sure that hope is a concept that would fit in because the whole practice is about being absolutely in the present moment. If we are in the present moment I am not sure we need hope except that it is the hope of finding the ability to truly BE in that present moment that may keep someone practicing the art of meditation and stillness for years."

These workplace riddles can't really be solved so much as pondered for their wisdom. "Living in the present" is an art of leadership, yet thinking we can ever be in anything other than the present is a mental error. Memory is present tense, as are aims and aspirations. Stuffing reality into a narrow category we call the here-and-now is to be overdetermined by what we think of as the present, and is perhaps another form of denial.

Denial is an insidious competitor with hope. A little denial may help us over the rough spots, but how much is too much, and how do we even know? Denial makes claims on reality of which we are unaware. It's always good for leaders to ask others whether they are "in denial," whether they're "missing something," or "not thinking straight," or "not getting the full story." Techniques to combat denial include 360-degree performance feedback, anonymous "hot lines," employee and customer surveys, "skip-level" meetings, and inviting unwelcome or opposing views. Hopeful organizations go out of their way to compete against the forces of denial, and they reward truth.

EVIL

This remarkable paragraph was offered by a respondent who is also a manager with international responsibilities:

> "I think that hope can exist concomitantly with fear and probably even with pessimism. In common discourse, pessimism is an inclination to expect the worst possible outcome. But does expecting that worst-case outcome really totally preclude believing that something better could occur? Not necessarily. It's more interesting if you think about pessimism philosophically—the doctrine that reality is basically evil or at least that evil is more than a match for happiness in the world. If you believe that, you better have hope. Or be willing to wait around for grace!"

Very few of the corporate citizens we interviewed had much to say about evil. Pessimism, fear, and denial yes, but not evil. Dan O'Neill, founder of MercyCorps, suggests, "there is a time to give up hope" (though not surrender to evil):

> "In conflict or violent situations, forgiveness must be extended at some level for the polarized parties to reach agreement. While the clinical definition of forgiveness is 'voluntarily giving up the desire to punish or hold resentment against another,' a more profound definition is 'giving up all hope for a better past.' It is frequently revenge that fuels cycles of violence, and revenge is based on 'getting even' for an event of the past."[28]

Within the corporate ethos, when you're faced with evil in the form of toxic behavior, you move on. Blowing the whistle is considered blowing it. So evil is downplayed as incompetence, and the hope (or is it surrender?) is that this too shall pass.

Karl Menninger, in 1959, named hope as "the enemy of evil."[29] Lance Morrow's compelling essay on evil, published in 2003, reached the same conclusion:

> "I think the opposite of evil is not good, but rather, hope—a more kinetic and practical thing. Evil, God knows, is energetic, and needs to be opposed by something more vigorous than 'good'...."

Morrow concludes with this thought: "Hope is the primary energy of the will to live, the will to survive."[30]

Desperate, without hope, people in extreme situations act, and in so doing, create hope.

Ronald Aronson

One lesson to be drawn from the Pandora story of hope is that it's human nature to be optimistic and curious, to take Pandora's gift and look beyond evil. "We want to be optimistic about our world and see the beauty; however the historical memory of evil is ignored at great cost."[31] The function of hope is to acknowledge the existence of evil. Unlike fear, evil is not a part of hope. Leaders need to be decisive and uncompromising in the face of malfeasance and grounded in their curiosity. Like Pandora, we are curious and naive, so let's not deny our nature.

Hope keeps us from overidentifying with the good, which is a form of naiveté, and from seeing ourselves other than as we really are. Leaders are just like us because they are us. Human, humble, humor, and humus all have the same linguistic roots in words meaning the organic portion of dirt.

Hope's Five Principles

We need to be wise in our handling of hope, as much as we need to be smart in our handling of reality.[1]

Maurice Lamm

"This is a turnaround. We haven't identified all the things that need to be fixed—no one here is a genius. We learn as we go." The speaker is the general manager at a U.S. factory. The assembled group is his extended management team, together in a downtown hotel meeting room to learn more about the company's direction and become better aligned.

During the ice-breaking segment at the start of the meeting, people introduce themselves with their complete names and reveal something personal about their backgrounds. It turns out that the group is entirely European in heritage: Polish, Irish, Welsh, Dutch, German, Italian, Lithuanian, Slovak, and Russian. We are seated around tables arranged in a big "U." The mood is expectant and slightly wary—the General Manager has been on board for six months, and this is the first time this group has met. It's highly unusual for any but the sales people to have a meeting outside the plant.

The financial report is so full of good news, however, that it can't help but soften the edges. "Something dramatic has happened." Millions of dollars of new business is rolling in. For the first time in its five-year history, the company is making money. And with regard to customers, "We're not the enemy anymore." As always, there are opportunities to make improvement in scrap, machine uptime, and safety. Yet progress is occurring on these fronts too.

Let's listen in to the low-key, plainspoken GM, and see what we can discern about what's going on and going right:

> "Now customers are coming to us, and we have to tell them, we can't take all your business. We can't produce at the price you need, so we need to be more realistic in creating customer expectations and negotiate terms and capabilities up front. This is better than taking the business and then asking, now what do we do?"

> "Managing our business means we'll play the game by the rules of the game, nothing illegal, unethical or immoral."

> "We need honesty. We put a man on a machine that he didn't know how to run and he said so—he's now getting training."

> "Tell me the truth. I can deal with the truth. No one gets fired or punished for telling the truth. We'll make mistakes. I make them everyday. We need to know what our mistakes are, learn from them and fix them."

> "Let's not fool ourselves about what we can do—a 5% profit goal would be 100% improvement over what we've already accomplished; 10% is unrealistic."

Large themes are embedded in these statements. As a way to make shared sense we asked the group to compare how things were six months previously, before the new GM had arrived on the scene, with today. We put a "Hope Scale" on the flipchart and asked people to weigh in. Here are the results:

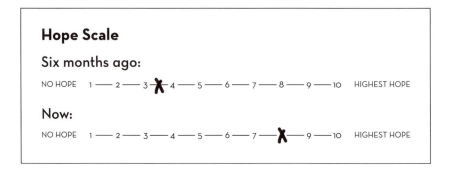

Hope Scale

Six months ago:

NO HOPE   1 — 2 — 3 —✗— 4 — 5 — 6 — 7 — 8 — 9 — 10   HIGHEST HOPE

Now:

NO HOPE   1 — 2 — 3 — 4 — 5 — 6 — 7 —✗— 9 — 10   HIGHEST HOPE

To learn more we asked everyone individually to provide an explanation. What's made the difference? After the meeting, we coded the responses according to the five principles of hope, about which we will have more to say in this section. Here are the verbatim responses as categorized:

Possibility

> "There's the potential for new markets and customers and to repair the damage of the past."

> "We have realistic management goals and stretch goals."

Agency

> "We buy-in."

> "There's common cause."

> "We can influence the future."

> "We're a piece of it now."

> "We control our own destiny."

Worth

> "We're still employed."

> "Results are good—sales are up."

Openness

> "Willingness to communicate."

> "There's honesty."

> "Open lines of communication."

Connection

> "Everyone is in the room when we make decisions."

> "Everyone is valued."

> "We actually have meetings!"

> "We get support when we ask for help."

> "We have exposure to customers."

> "We have a clear picture of jobs and roles."

Then there was this comment that didn't fit easily into one of the five buckets but seemed to cross all five principles: "There's strong energy in the group." When all five principles are present, something synaptic happens—hope fires hope.

In our original, early 1990s formulation "in the company of hope," we said hope is "an act that generates movement toward a shared, desirable future." Now, based upon our ethnographic research plus advances in the hope field, we broaden the earlier definition to include more than actions and collective outcomes: *hope is an orientation to a positive future that engages our heads, hearts and hands.*

According to the researchers Averill, Catlin, and Chon, when an individual is faced with a situation where "rules of hope" really do apply, that person usually "can't help" but hope."[2] Our belief is that when the five principles of hope are present at work, *and when they're sustained*, individuals and their organizations "can't help" but achieve positive results.

"And the dim fluorescent lighting is meant to emphasize the general absence of hope."

Chapter 5

Possibility

Gone, or almost, is the type [of person] who once sought to combine reason and hope, a gritty sense of limits with a lofty sense of possibility.[1]

Ronald Aronson

The New England Center for Children (NECC) is a prize-winning school using applied behavior analysis—an art of the possible—to make progress with seemingly impossible cases of autism and other developmental disabilities. In brief, NECC was founded in 1975 to provide state-of-the-art education and individualized treatment "with care and respect" for children with autism and other related disabilities. Concretely, this mission has meant two things. First, NECC has avoided aversive, punishment-based methods, and has kept its dedication to positive, reinforcing modes of treatment, and "respect for the dignity and individuality of each child" as its core value. Second, NECC has ignored "cure du jour" approaches to treating children with autism, and uses only proven scientific methods and programs. Thus, it educates the student with autism while providing support and training to sustain the family.

As a result, NECC has established a reputation as one of the premier schools of its type in the world. It now serves more than 200 students between the ages of 2 and 22 from across the United States and from several foreign countries. Staff, numbering in the hundreds, have been recognized around the world—NECC has earned the National Award for Model Professional Development from the U.S. Department of Education, the only private school ever to receive the award, and the 2005 award from the Society for the Advancement of Behavioral Analysis for Enduring Programmatic Contributions to Behavior Analysis. NECC's basic and applied research has been published in over a hundred articles in scientific journals. Furthermore, NECC staff are regularly chosen from among their peers for awards and recognition, such as *Exceptional Parent Magazine*'s "Best of the Best Direct Support Professionals." Not surprisingly, there is a long waitlist for students.

NECC stands as a shining example of hope's principle of possibility. Autism is not curable—that is impossible. Autism is treatable, however, and with assistance, children with autism can make a tremendous amount of progress.

NECC really knows what it is doing. First, NECC knows applied behavioral analysis, the only proven method, and it doesn't stray. Second, NECC sticks to its values of respect for individuals. Third, NECC is rigorous in selecting, training, and retaining the best teachers it can find. And finally, NECC chooses its students very carefully. Student selection is based partly on whether their families are supportive and not given to impose their own philosophies of treatment. Students are mostly chosen at an early-enough age where their disabilities, though severe, are within the realm of possibility to benefit the most from treatment.

Note first that challenging goals are established each year and baked into management plans reviewed by the board of directors. There are goals for every area of the school: student progress, staff development, professional contribution, community outreach, and institutional growth. Goal targets stretch limits yet stay within reach.

Second, there is flexibility in how goals are achieved. Applied behavior analysis, the core teaching method at NECC, is a disciplined approach yet not so rigid that teachers are prevented from exercising creativity. Kathy Foster, the Associate Executive Director explains:

> "There is leeway in figuring out what will work with each individual child and then to determine what teaching approach will work best. For example, you could use a 'shaping approach' of successive approximation to teach writing letters, or you could use 'hand-over-hand guidance and physical fading,' and there are many other choices.

> "The staff use universal principles of learning and apply them according to the learning history of each child.

> "Results are measured in a continuous feedback loop. Currently, 83.4% of our students made progress or met their individual education objectives."

Moreover, management goals for financial growth as well as the furtherance of programmatic excellence call out for constant innovation and simultaneous effort. The orientation toward results at NECC, no matter what the point of departure is—what is known as "equifinality" in the biological sciences—enables success.

THE CHALLENGE OF STRETCHING LIMITS

The word "possibility" comes from the Latin root "posse," meaning to be able, to be powerful, and to be feasible. It is related to the word "potential," the capacity for growth and development. Possibility encompasses the creative dreamer in us who can imagine and the realist who knows that hope is passion for the possible. Or as one of our respondents put it, "A jump start feeds on itself." So hope is neither a walk in the park nor a dive into the unknown.

Said another way, the relationship between hope and probability is curvilinear—hope concerns events that are neither assured nor impossible.[2] When what you hope for is out of sight and felt to be impossible to achieve, you feel doubtful about whether to make an effort. Conversely, when what you hope for is sure-fire and guaranteed, there's no reason to hope in the first place. It's wasted breath, pointless, and your efforts aren't really needed. The principle of possibility states that you hope best when you hope for something in the range of what you see as being possible.

> Possibilities
>
> *One brick,*
> *Lying on the sidewalk.*
> *It could be a house,*
> *It could be a building,*
> *It could be used to build*
> *A stairway*
> *To heaven.*
> *It could be used to build*
> *A hospital.*
> *The possibilities are endless,*
> *For that one brick,*
> *It could be anything*
> *When somebody finds it,*
> *But now it's just a brick,*
> *Lying on the sidewalk.*
>
> *Kalliope Rodman Dalto, Age 9,*
> *Barbara's Granddaughter*

"The beginning of hope is defining an audacious goal. It feels hard, chaotic initially. Possibility creates coping, coming to grips. You go from possibility to an oh-my-god moment when you connect possibility to agency."

Many of our respondents described the sweet spot of possibility—setting goals with just the right degree of stretch to inspire hope:

"My new boss inspires me. He helped us all develop stretch goals by asking us to write an article for the *Harvard Business Review* describing the future of the business from ten years out. It was freeing to create our hopes and vision in journalistic terms, not a business plan. It allowed me to dream big, to believe I could and that I was backed up with resources. The goals were almost impossible to believe. It's so easy to go for incrementalism. He set the bar high then let me come up with my own goal. It was not imposed, so I always believed it was doable."

The new boss evidently knows a thing or two about hopeful motivation; he tapped into the strengths of his associate and created a passion for the possible. Believing even an "audacious" goal is achievable helps people keep their balance as they take chances outside their comfort zones.

"People look for consistency more than perfection. People can live with 80/20. We believe the goals are achievable. Feeling challenged and not overwhelmed is a fine line."

The task of leadership is to "frame possibility and define success in ways that describe reality while dreaming." "The challenge, for the leader is to get folks to dream about the possible, to find their voice, stretching limits." There is a price to pay, however, for going beyond what is achievable:

"If we stretch beyond the possible, we get whacked. When I first started, the company saw no limits, no boundaries: if we can dream it we can do it. I never want to stop thinking that way, but I have to learn current limits, be sure things are possible. Maybe we need a 20-year plan."

Too much stretch creates a vicious cycle of dream and lose, dream again and lose again—a fine line walked by leaders who see possibility more audaciously than the rest of the organization:

"The new boss came into our top management meeting, and said 'We're going to capture 60% share of the business in 3 years.' We had 38%. Reaction: people were mad. This guy has no clue. This is impossible. He never wavered. He was a hard-nosed guy. We had to solve for it, and did."

The key element in this example is the level of hopefulness of the new boss. The psychologist of hope, C. Rick Snyder, revised his theory in this regard. People with truly high hope, as observed in his laboratory, "occasionally alter those seemingly absolute failure situations so as to attain the impossible.[3] Perhaps the new boss's resolve was matched by hope, or perhaps the 60% target wasn't as difficult as expected, or perhaps he got lucky.

Having a plan and the resources to back up possibility is the hopeful path forward. Without a substantive plan behind them, stretch goals can be naive and even dangerous. This is equivalent to making an investment without an exit plan, or launching a project without naming a deliverable result. "Others won't flock if the goal looks unrealistically aggressive. Show me the plan!"

Finally, involving the organization in establishing and aligning goals builds community expectations and also support. When goals are kept offline or under wraps, it is hard to celebrate when they are achieved—or feel too badly if they are missed. "When we talk about potential and possibility, it shifts the energy and mood. Hope then feels more public."

MULTIPLE SOLUTIONS

In an ethnographic study of innovation, we went out to hear stories from people within selected companies around the world in order to compare the most innovative firms with the rest. Stories carry the bedrock norms and values of a culture. One of the most compelling themes that emerged is that in really innovative companies the stories told are generative tales of how someone succeeded, perhaps against enormous odds, or how someone else took a big risk and wasn't made to suffer consequences. These operationally enabling stories teach parables of possibility, widening the space for innovative solutions.

In the less-than-innovative companies, the stories told around the coffee pot tended toward "ain't it awful": who got shot down, why it's too hard to make things happen, and how to keep a low profile. These operationally disabling stories teach parables of woe, frustration, and giving up, narrowing the scope of action.

The principle of possibility joins stretch goals with the prospect of many ways to accomplish them. Hope rests on knowing that a system can find new ways to discover and mine new opportunities. Here are themes we discovered, in the language of our respondents:

Establish Common Ground

The theme of getting broad understanding and buy-in to stretch goals was clear. "You can't stretch limits unless there's common ground," said one respondent. Another said,

> "The leader has to provide possibility, being as inclusive as possible. In our strategic planning process, 100 managers, bottom up, learned and were part of the plan. Everyone bought in, engaged and participating—necessary to understand the context of decisions."

As for a third, "It can start with the essentials: a sense of possibility linked to a clear vision of the outcome longed for."

For years, Marvin Weisbord and Sandra Janoff have been advocating large group meeting structures where representatives from a full range of an organization's stakeholders are present and participating. By design, these "Future Search Conferences" are positive responses to traditional planning sessions where people focus on problems and create long lists of things to, with the result feeling "hopeless."[4] In Chapter 6 we will describe several Future Search Conferences we've managed. For now, it is important to emphasize the value of establishing "common ground" as an underlying basis.

As an example, it was reported recently that two old friends and foes, the conservative pope Cardinal Joseph Ratzinger and the liberal dissident theologian Rev. Hans Kung, had met and found "common ground." Although both were once liberals and friends, they diverged in their views during student unrest in Germany in the 1960s—Rev. Kung became a critic of papal infallibility and was later banned from teaching. Their conversations ranged far and wide on topics such as the role of the church in a secular world and the relationship between science and religion, and they released a statement afterward that was written by the pope and "approved every word" by Rev. Kung, who reported: "It is a sign of hope for many Catholics and for many people in the world that two so different people as we nevertheless agreed on so many things with regard to the future of the world."[5]

Weisbord writes that Future Search Conferences stake out "the widest *common ground* all can stand on—hearing and appreciating differences, identifying but not reconciling polarities—to "learn, innovate and act from a mutual base of discovered ideals, world views, and future goals." So common ground is a hopeful place, a platform where a purposeful group can "stick to business."[6]

Be Confident

Hope "has a lot to do with your self-confidence, belief in self and those around you":

> "Maybe you have to kid yourself a little. There's an overwhelming amount of choices, directions, possibilities. I have to feel good about myself and take a reality check."

Another said, we had "great confidence because we banded together as a team; we believe the goals we set are achievable. We embarked on the possibility as one."

Rosabeth Moss Kantor, whose recent book is entitled *Confidence*, defines confidence as neither optimism, pessimism nor a character attribute, but "the expectation of a positive outcome." And she proffers this advice to build or regain confidence: focus on milestones to big results. "Small wins can improve the odds of bigger successes later on."[7]

Take a Stand

One leader told us: "The first step is taking control of one's destiny and believing in oneself." Another said, "Don't go for out-of-scope. Treat commitment as important." And a third respondent said,

> "You take a stand in a possibility. We all know it. It's inspiring. We play it back to our vendors in all our communication, and it's backed up by putting resources into innovation."

For someone else, "If I know where you are and there's a positive, clear, articulate vision, the difference creates potential energy." Taking a hopeful stand means putting your stake in the ground—and being prepared to move it. As part of the process, lest we lose our balance, we need to narrow "the gap between what we hope and what is true."[8]

Enroll and Align

"Enrollment, alignment—when we're all involved in the creation of the goal it takes on reality and becomes possible. To be creative, you have to create the context." Context appears as a larger frame than numbers: "Most people are not excited by financial goals. They want to be part of a winning team," said one respondent. Another agreed:

> "Unrealistic goals tied solely to financials are enervating. Goals should be based on other values besides money. Black and white is not inspiring."

A way forward is to "help people see analogous situations to see that hope is there. People love to hang onto examples."

In their book on nonprofit leadership, Barry Dym and Harry Hutson define alignment as "the fundamental act of leadership in organizations."[9] Leaders perform acts of alignment in both their everyday practices of connecting people, strategy and effort, and through formal planning and monitoring processes. They also warn about overalignment that eliminates creative friction. Hopeful organizations are not always conflict-free—and they're never complacent.

Get Real

"False hope is fantasy. Even discontinuous goals have to be grounded in reality." So even with an extended timeframe, things need to happen now: "Our mission will take 5–10 years, reachable in our work lifetime, yet we can see things move."

One of the most hopeful practices to handle stretch goals is to break them down into subgoals, to "chunk" them. For years, the consultant Robert Schaffer has advised his clients about how to achieve "breakthroughs" by building on short-term successes.[10] The method is based on goals that meet the following five criteria:

1. They are urgent and compelling.
2. First steps are achievable in the near term.
3. There is a "bottom-line" result at stake—an outcome that is discrete, measurable, and important.
4. Those responsible are good to go—engaged, committed, and competent.
5. The resources needed to do the job are already available.

Schaffer's strategy has been put to the test in many organizations to make improvements of every kind: creating new products and processes, rooting out wasteful costs, smoothing internal procedures, increasing customer satisfaction, and more. It is a simple yet effective method to "get real" about possibility.

Get Moving

Jo Luck, president and CEO of Heifer International, has said, "Without hope you can't succeed and with it you can do anything—but you've got to have resources." and there must also be "specific action, seeing initial success."[11] Another leader said: "Possibility for the sake of possibility is a trap. Dreaming is not moving the enterprise forward."

Other respondents offered similar wisdom along the lines of "get moving so more can happen." Hopeful movement provides, in the words of a manager, an "opportunity to grow, stretch, flex muscles, see different sides of ourselves, be courageous and be boxed in." Another respondent used these words: "If you open yourself to possibility it's more likely to happen and you make your own luck." As yet another told us, "Life gets on paths, and then a door opens up . . . ."

Hope is the dream of a soul awake.

French Proverb

THE ART OF POSSIBILITY

We hope for what we now have, only different and better. So we adjust our expectations according to our estimates of likelihood. The task is to determine the art of the possible. "What gives me hope about our new direction is that next year will be harder and that the next year (after that) will be even harder." Whether this "new direction" can deliver hope on a broad scale will depend on the ability of leadership to master the art of possibility. Another manager told us that the "mindset of possibility is powerful day and night in terms of innovation, and it multiplies chances of success by an order of magnitude." As Averill, Catlin, and Chon have suggested, for possibility to be meaningful in any setting, it must not be a necessity. There must be room to maneuver. Furthermore, human beings must be alive with possibility. "With hope, we begin to realize the possibilities inherent in both the situation and in ourselves."[12]

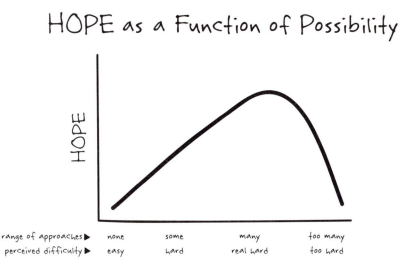

To review the main points, the principle of possibility has two dimensions, both conforming to the hopeful, golden mean. First, goals must stretch the limits of what is seen as possible. When you stretch limits, moreover, you *respect* limits. Dreaming the impossible dream is motivational for very few of us. At the other extreme, untested limits offer the vast majority of us little in the way of personal satisfaction. Hope begins when you consider going beyond the normal and routine.

Second, goals must invite multiple solutions. Too many possibilities, however, create chaos and confusion and can encourage random choices, or have the paradoxical effect of inhibiting choice-making altogether. Barry Schwartz writes that "living at the pinnacle of human possibility" has a steep price attached: psychological distress.[13] We spend our lives making choices that mean little and end up making us less, not more happy. In a world of proliferating choices, clearly more is less. Then to go all the way in the other direction, having too few possibilities confines us to the tried-and-true and stifles imagination.

Gareth Morgan, who invented the word "imaginization" to describe the process of infusing management with imagination, writes how "it is impossible to develop new styles of organization and management while continuing to think in old ways."[14] Our "futureblocks," as he calls them, include all those things that get in the way of hope, and especially any self-limiting images we hold of ourselves. The principle of possibility, therefore, is the art of thinking in new ways that aren't self-limited—foundational for the practice of leadership.

Chapter 6

Agency

Hope can flourish only when you believe that what you do can make a difference, that your actions can bring a future different from the present.[1]

Jerome Groopman

The Avery Dennison factory in Juarez, Mexico is a sight to see, but that was not always the case. Before 2000, it was just another of the hundreds of *maquiladoras* created by U.S. companies to manufacture more in Mexico. This one makes office products. A manager who remembers visiting the plant in 1999, when there were 2,000 associates, said "you couldn't see the people! Boxes of material were everywhere, and the place was a mess." Things are different today. Since 2000, the operation has been transformed, and the story speaks to principle of agency within the context of hope.

Today there are fewer people than there were in 2000—natural attrition has allowed significant gains in productivity—and the business has made dramatic improvement in measurable results: sales, service, profit, worker turnover and morale, and world-class safety. Even the plant soccer teams (men's and women's) are winning. The images formed on a recent walk-through are memorable:

Spacious aisles, clean machines, shiny floors, well-lit and brightly painted work areas, spotless cafeteria, orderly offices.

Visual clues everywhere: safety rules, where things belong, how to operate machines, who won recent awards and contests, upcoming events, menus, photographs of workers at team events and celebrations, operational results, targets and expectations, who belongs to which team, evaluations of participation and satisfaction at events, display cases of products on the factory floor.

People in groups at work cells running operations in what can only be described as a natural rhythm—confident, smiling, relaxed—people in training sessions learning English, people busy in offices willing to help explain things, people in shift-wide exercise sessions, people purposeful and on the go.

How has this been accomplished? Let's identify a number of factors and then tie them together under the theme of agency. First, they do what they say. One of the plant's distinctive core values is "Optimism: We believe in our capacity and readiness to fulfill our commitments." The plant's vision includes this line with statements about business leadership: "To create opportunities and development where our personnel feel proud, sure and motivated." When Javier Villalobos became site manager in 2000, he started the turnaround by launching an orderliness and cleanliness program where it now seems obvious to start: "at the top, in the offices." The point was not lost on the factory floor, and when it was their turn the operators became fully engaged in cleaning and painting and organizing. There were positive competitions with recognition, photos, banners, and lunches. The before-and-after pictures are now shown with great pride.

There was a Saturday during the busiest production season when Javier stopped work to continue the orderliness and cleanliness program. This was a courageous decision in a numbers-driven environment, but Javier knew what he was doing. He traded off a short-term goal for long-term gain. Housekeeping and safety are fundamental to establishing a culture of commitment.

Next, rapid improvement events were launched where workers would stop production and spend several intense days solving problems, eliminating blockages, or setting up better ways to do their jobs. Now there are eighty of these events a year, but in the beginning Javier had to take a risk to get them started. Rapid improvement events were new to the company, and they disrupted routines. Yet Javier persisted, and the Juarez facility has become a model site for these best practices in worker engagement.

One of their winning ideas is how progress is measured and checked. Every work cell is audited every week on just five key metrics (less is more), and the audit teams are composed of a cross-section of people from all levels of the organization. That way, people can learn from each other and spread good ideas throughout the plant. Rewards and recognition—with banners—are a part of every weekly audit.

Meanwhile, building a culture of operations improvement—a culture of agency—has taken place within the larger context of Mexican culture and society. The Avery Dennison *maquila* in Juarez is one of the few with

Mexican leadership. The highly educated leadership team (90% have masters' degrees in business or engineering, and all of them have certifications in the Six Sigma improvement process), has made education and training a priority for the workforce. There are continual sessions and courses and publications and videos and town meetings on a host of topics, and there is even a plant library. Holidays such as Dia de la Raza are celebrated in a big way. There is even a system of goals and objectives that touches every hourly person—everyone matters at Juarez.

Perhaps what is most core to success is the degree to which the whole person is affirmed and attended to. The orderliness and cleanliness program that began with a focus on things and needs has been expanded in a unique way to include people. Four of the nine priorities concern personal issues: well-being (health, attitude, recreation, family harmony), training and discipline (personal habits and rules), constancy ("try, try, and try many times"), and commitment ("to do something").

When the current site manager Antonio Cano first arrived, he was confident in being able to pick things up and move forward. First, he would savor "the potential of the moment." Later, as an act of hope, he would create a "positive crisis."

AGENCY FUELS ACTION

"Hope does not always fuel action," according to the leadership coach, Sandy Davis. "It is usually the other way around. Clear intentions and purposeful action fuel hope." Sandy has it right. In the Juarez factory, where intentions are closely connected to actions, people at every level feel responsible to make choices. They are *agents*, positive actors in their own lives as well as in the life of the plant. We want to highlight two factors that undergird their high degree of agency: they have the motivation to do their jobs as well as they can, and they are supported in their efforts by the organization and its leaders.

According to our interview respondents, these themes play out in all manner of work settings. Here are some choice comments, first with regard to leadership:

"A change agent has to be passionate because he or she will get beat up. Not everyone along the food chain is similarly passionate."

"Our leader let us know challenging him was OK. Junior people became part of the decision process. That's like throwing kerosene on a fire, a great confidence builder."

"I'd rather you call me and say X went ahead without me than that X won't move. I'd prefer to rein you in than spur you on."

"Leadership needed is not patriarchal but energized and empowered."

"Our organizational structure is complicated, and that could be a limiting factor. A new brand manager came in and said he wouldn't let it limit us. He took action, pushed people to make decisions."

"Leadership means getting people to take initiative versus protecting their turf."

"I tend to undervalue my contribution/voice. Some of my people don't realize the value of theirs. It's the responsibility of the leader to point that out."

"The attitude 'we are the leaders we have been waiting for ...' feeds on itself in a positive cycle."

On taking responsibility:

"The core of my definition of hope: taking personal responsibility."

"In one of our big plants, a line worker shut the line down. The plant manager asked, 'Who gave you the authority?' 'Roger (the CEO) did,' came the reply. 'He said we're going to make quality a reality.'"

> *I will act as if what I do makes a difference.*
>
> *William James*

"You have to choose hope, choose to see the possibilities. In hard times, that's a hard choice to make in the morning. It requires taking personal responsibility and ownership and being empowered. Not giving up."

"We had a goal but didn't know how to get there, so we challenged ourselves and did a lot of consumer work. We went from wondering if this was a crazy goal to knowing we can succeed."

"There are moments of truth, little decisions everyday—many opportunities to take action regardless of the level."

"Hope inspires action: What action can you take today?"

"Part and parcel of being hopeful is the serenity prayer: grant me the courage to change those things that I can change, the serenity to accept those things I cannot, and the wisdom to realize the difference between the two. Thus, being agentic sometimes means letting go."

"Hope means efficacy and feeling on the mark and in the zone, in individuals and teams. This can be opportunistic: 'I'm going to get away with this!' or 'We are on top and going to win!' Or it can be altruistic: 'I can do this and it will help!'"

"If you've been charged with contributing to an organization because it aspires to be 'the best,' you know what your contribution can be. You have power. It fills your hope bucket."

On being included:

"People want to be part of a winning team. The barrier is if their ideas are not heard, thanked, appreciated, and understood—then they're not giving their best."

"Professionalism is valuing everyone's point of view, and then we make a contribution."

"I need personal connection to be inspired."

"The human condition's worst fear is a life of insignificance, leaving no footprint. We want to be part of something."

"You have to tell people how meaningful their work is."

"Inclusion means tops, middles, bottoms—all understanding how to contribute."

"Signs of agency: how many decisions I get pulled into."

"Being included makes people feel they have a piece of the rock and provides a good reason to get up in the morning feeling excited."

On barriers to agency:

"Agency is something to strive for in a perfect world. I'm amazed at the personal time it takes to achieve. It's not a natural leadership trait for all managers, and not a way all like to be managed."

Men often oppose a thing merely because they have had no agency in planning it, or because it may have been planned by those whom they dislike.

Alexander Hamilton

"Big companies need approachability in the hierarchy to encourage experimentation."

"We need the freedom of a start-up where there's room for risk."

"There's perceived risk: fear, cynicism, and managers who aren't bought-in. We've been highly controlled for so long. Now the organization puts out a lofty goal, but how do you really do that?"

"Standing still is not an option."

"This organization's culture works against agency. We manage the biggest projects but are not given our budgets. There's no control or information. It's parent/child."

"To the extent I don't feel agency I don't feel hope."

In summary, agency sounds like this:

"You can make a difference no matter where in the organization."

"With the right level of support, even if you're not a risk taker, you may be willing to take a chance."

"At the heart of it: something you can do, concrete steps, having a plan."

SEARCHING FOR AGENCY

Commitment to action begins with voice—having a voice in discovering and planning the future, being the change versus being changed. In our experience, one of the most powerful tools for generating agency is the Future Search Conference, a powerful strategic planning meeting designed to discover and explore common ground.

The conference itself is typically quite large—sixty or more people representing different constituencies whose voices and commitment are vital to analyzing the past and present and planning for the future. During the three-day conference, the group will develop a shared understanding of forces affecting their context, their current responses, and how they want to respond in the future. They also have a chance to think through the kinds of relationships they want to have among various players in the coming months and years.

Participants work on various activities in small, self-managed groups to pool ideas, analyze information, and present conclusions to the whole conference. Participants create desired future scenarios that become joint property of all. Each group then has a chance to consider how these scenarios are likely to affect their own planning over the next few years and how they can contribute to the overall effort.

Marvin Weisbord and Sandra Janoff, champions of the Future Search Conference movement, have said that these meetings make possible, in a few days, planning breakthroughs thought previously impossible. People make great progress despite past conflict and diverse perspectives. There have been thousands of these conferences around the world managed by community-based nonprofits, educational institutions, corporations, and multiagency national initiatives.[2]

The principle of agency is embedded in the design of these meetings by bringing together the "whole system," a cross-section of key stakeholders

Hope does not mean dreaming on about the future. Hope means aiming at it and refusing to believe you cannot make it.

Maurice Lamm

who will take an active part in formulating strategy and plans. They are not mere bystanders; they are people who must feel a sense of personal ownership for the session's outcomes. Agency comes from involvement in the planning process and the hope that propels a community toward action. Under such circumstances actual implementation of initiatives is much more likely.

We have led many such conferences. What is most notable in the context of corporate cultures is the opportunity to have, in one room, a cross-section of multiple levels and functions, "the whole system" working together "on a level playing field" to envision and plan their future.

We managed three Future Search Conferences for the operations function of Fannie Mae, the home mortgage financial giant. Their goal was to transform people, processes, and structure from the "back-office mentality" of a bureaucracy to an agentic, team-based, and flexible organization that could support the corporation's goals for the future. According to one of the leaders:

"The value added here was the buy-in of all participants as agents of change. To reengineer the company we will have to change the culture, and WE are the culture. It will take time, but let's begin to live the changes."

The most striking thing about this effort was that the process of bringing together management and rank-and-file employees to talk together on an equal footing was culturally groundbreaking for a hierarchical organization. In the words of one participant, "I felt the inclusion of people at all levels was quite empowering.... The evolution of Fannie Mae is a big project." The inclusive design of the meeting in terms of both attendees and activities broadcast that Agency, on everyone's part, was the way forward.

Another example of a Future Search Conference we managed was named "Mapping the Future of the Pacific Crest Trail." The PCT, one of America's longest hiking trails, connects Canada and Mexico along the spine of the Cascades and Sierras. For three days, we were a diverse group of stakeholders who had never before come together—hikers and equestrians, Federal agencies, trail associations, community, and board members—working together to plan for the future of the trail and to put ourselves into those plans. In the words of Jim Hilton, then President of the Pacific Crest Trail Association:

"This is the greatest collection of people interested in the trail that has ever been put together. The work that comes together here will potentially be important to all trail systems, not just our own."

The result was a realistic, collective set of goals and action plans. Many at the conference left personally committed to carrying out ambitious projects that were developed and to ensuring their success.

The impact of the meeting is very much alive according to Liz Bergeron, Executive Director of the PCTA: "A few of the work groups have tackled projects this past year with little or no staff input. For a volunteer organization such as ours, this is exactly the kind of commitment we need in order to reach our goals."

SUSTAINING AGENCY

Heifer International is an agency that builds agency. As the story goes, it was founded by a Midwestern farmer named Dan West who was ladling milk to children in the Spanish Civil War when the thought struck him: "These children don't need a cup, they need a cow."

West formed Heifers for Relief—the first cows left Pennsylvania for Puerto Rico in 1944, and now Heifer International is a worldwide effort that has served millions of families in 115 countries. The three components are livestock (cows, pigs, chickens, sheep, goats, horses . . .), training and extension work with families, and an organized method to "passing on the gifts." The compelling idea is agency on a global scale: helping hungry people feed themselves.

The livestock received by families and communities is considered a "living loan" to be repaid by donating offspring. Thus, the process is self-sustaining both in economic and human terms, one family, one animal at a time. Heifer abjures temporary relief and handouts in favor of "securing a future with generations of people who have hope, health and dignity."

It's striking how the Heifer formula provides a recipe for agency—and hope. In stark terms, poor people are alleviating the poverty of other poor people. And as a result, over the project's sixty years, 7 million families and 38 million individuals have been served.

Jo Luck, President and CEO of Heifer International, tells the story of a recent visit to Kenya and (this was not her purpose) exemplifies leadership behavior that encourages agency:

"We went to Eastern Kenya, an HIV-AIDS affected area, to a remote community to understand how to work with blind people in the field. You talk about hope! They love to have a reason to celebrate. I'm standing with dignitaries as a group of 22, mostly women, come forward to sing for us.

"A gentleman said, there's Grace. Last week we went to her bed—she was dying. It's definitely the goat she got from Heifer: the milk saved her, and she used money from the milk to buy her medicines."

"They were singing the names of people who've died in the last 30 days. The stories they sing tell people to have hope. Only people who are HIV-positive are in the choir.

"Then we went to areas where people are blind. Children learn to take care of the animals after two or three years of training. An older, blind gentleman who had taken the training showed me the animals in a pen (a cow, goat and chickens). He had planted a field and fertilized it and improved his house and educated the children. It was a long and exhausting day, yet it was exhilarating.

"They had hope—you can't succeed without it, and with it you can do anything, but you have to have resources, and you have to be connected in your heart. By itself, buying goats does not a new life make."[3]

A colleague described the following in his trip report:

"Jo Luck speaks to supporters and donors on the wonderful work Heifer International does by giving hope to desperate people and Nam Jai [a Laotian term that means 'living waters of the heart'—compassion, hope, and spirituality] at heart. She speaks on their behalf. In order that she has full knowledge of the very poor people and be able to speak authoritatively on their behalf, she has to come to meet them, speak with them, eat with them and rejoice with them when an activity is successful.... She has to recharge her knowledge by visiting the recipients of Heifer assistance and her Nam Jai through field visits. The above trip fulfilled that objective, as I believe Jo Luck went back to Little Rock more recharged than she came out."[4]

Note the virtuous circle of agency. Heifer International is all about people doing things for themselves, and Jo Luck as an "agent of agency" returns from an exhausting trip to the field with renewed energy.

MAKING THINGS HAPPEN

The principle of agency is our willing involvement and participation in a collective endeavor, where we have both the will and desire and also adequate resources. When we feel truly *agentic*, we turn ourselves from bystanders into actors. Agency is the difference between wishful thinking and hope, where we move up the scale from seeing something that needs to be done to doing it.

Our mental, physical, and spiritual energy is most engaged when we are included in planning and making decisions about issues that affect us. When we are left out, we may go along with the program but not with the same kind of energy had we been able to influence the course of events. There are two points as follows.

Agency in a Range of Hopefulness

First, in a work environment where one person takes over, agency deteriorates—we want to get out of the way. Sometimes it's "leading by example," but if the takeover style continues indefinitely and fails to empower others, it degenerates into "doing it myself." Fanaticism is the extreme example of this phenomenon, and it can be repellant. And at the other end, in a work setting where everyone is held responsible but no one is specifically accountable, agency is weakened in a different way. Apathy reigns, and people are indifferent. What's the point of exerting myself?—it's not my job. In either case, collective will and desire to succeed are severely compromised, and concerted action in the group is unlikely.

And second, when there are too few resources to get the job done, our best efforts are starved. That may be obvious, but what is less obvious and just as hopeless is having too *many* resources. When organizations are in the start-up mode, for example, if there is too much money available to the management team thanks to overenthusiastic investors, the temptation is to spend it. Furthermore, big budgets can cause mistakes such as paying consultants to do your thinking or paying outsiders to do work that is core to your business. Bad enough, but too many resources too easily secured can create entitlement. So either way, when resources are either inadequate or too generous, agency suffers.

The entrepreneur Ginny O'Brien says, "For me professionally, in terms of growing my business, hope is always about seeing the possibility of something happening in the future, about believing that I can make things happen." The principle of agency unleashes not only our hope but also our commitment and willingness to think creatively and work hard toward goals we really care about.

Chapter 7

Worth

Far and away the best prize that life offers is the chance to work hard at work worth doing.[1]

Theodore Roosevelt

A fact not well known is that falling down is the beginning of chronic illness that is often irreversible—much depends on whether you can get help quickly. Lifeline Systems, Inc. is one of several companies offering twenty-four-hour monitoring and personalized support to elderly subscribers as well as to physically challenged individuals, and it's very good at what it does: building *worth* for its clients and customers, its associates and stakeholders. Their mission is to work with healthcare providers, social service organizations, referral networks, and caregivers "to provide personal response services to the at-risk elderly to enhance their independence and quality of life and to help them remain in their own homes."

Lifeline is the preferred provider of personal response systems to members of the Visiting Nurse Associations of America, the American Red Cross, and thousands of hospitals. It has a strong marketing base, a proven business model, capable leadership, and excellent growth prospects, and it wins prizes: for growth (*Inc Magazine*'s Fastest Growing, among others), for quality (Shingo Prize), and for service (American Society on Aging's "Business of the Year"). It has also set the unusual example of a company that has "in-sourced" jobs back home after having outsourced them offshore.

Lifeline's people—those who take the calls and who create the systems and structures that make it all possible—are the true added value in the equation. They are passionate and competent. And they are well aware that what they do affects peace of mind and the quality of life. Here is a typical endorsement:

> "My mother, who is 80 and lives alone, fell. Thankfully, she was wearing a Lifeline pendant, which she activated, and within five minutes, help was on the way. I don't know how I could ever have peace of mind without their service."

Two sets of images emerge from a visit to Lifeline. First, the company is focused on its mission. The main building is decorated with hundreds of life-size photographs of clients—elderly persons, often with their children, spouses, or caregivers, smiling for the camera or just going about their business—so the message is clear. Second, the company is successful, and it feels it. People are busy, engaged, polite, and on a roll. While earnest about tasks at hand, they anticipate meeting the next company milestone and enjoying the next celebration.

Lifeline is a feel-good story in a feel-good business, but with a tough skeleton of values underneath—a company that "does good *and* does well." Ron Feinstein, who is the CEO, offers several insights. At Lifeline there is a deliberate path that starts with company values concerning relationships—loyalty, passion, respect, care, and learning—proceeding to technology and service, and then finding a way to a special place in the market. Feinstein says,

> "It's a living core values system. People are responsive. People work hard here. It's a values-based company."

Yet, along with affirmative values, according to Feinstein, there is clarity and sanction:

> "It's as if we're training to run the Boston Marathon. We're determined to be successful. The mindset is being focused and determined and having great clarity about the journey and end-game.
>
> "I'm not out there to contain or set limits or manage as much as I'm trying to bring great clarity to values that exist here. People can be who they'll be within our core values. Those who don't embrace caring and respect for one another, or continuous improvement and quality are conspicuous."

Although a case can be made that Lifeline provides hope to clients, and that many of Lifeline's associates are indeed hopeful people, the word hope has never been used. "We've been at this for a long time," says Feinstein, and "we take years before we write things down." Words are measured very carefully at Lifeline, and they're rooted in experience. "Hard copy is an early sign of failure."

This glimpse into Lifeline suggests that winning values—the sense of worth that permeates collective activity—are hard won. The principle of worth is essential to creating a positive future at work, whether or not the word hope is part of the conversation. When leaders focus on doing what is most worthwhile they enhance organizational meaning and motivation.

NOT A SURPRISE

One of the "surprise" findings of a group of social scientists who surveyed the literature of hope was that "hope is almost always portrayed as having a moral, spiritual, or religious dimension."[2] This is not a surprise for us—worth was a constant theme in our interviews. Cliff Hakim, who is a writer, career consultant, and speaker, said it this way:

"HOPE is present for me when I feel that my work is personally meaningful, when my work strikes a deep internal cord and I have a sense that my focus is a concern and yearning for others, too. For example, my zeal has been to 'focus on what counts' in life. As we mature, we learn that life is short: there's little time to waste."

Darkness is not all,
Nor war the last word;
Not by a long shot, or a short.
The children speak it;
The last word. Hope.
Hope; the children.
The child.

Yehuda Amichai

Sense of worth, as a principle of hope, is always both meaningful and motivational, and it works on every level of life. Here are five of our respondents speaking about what is most important to them:

"My daughter came to a meeting with me then said, 'I want to be you.' For me, it's the legacy I leave my family and kids. I get up in the morning and I want to go to work, intrinsically."

"For me it's tied to overall vision and mission. We're enriching the home, not selling dishes. It's the emotional content of our brand, the relationship with the consumers who love our product. That's the true worth of this company. I get all excited when I think like a consumer and never let up."

"It's more than just company, money, and share growth. It's personal—the worth of the team—and it's self-reinforcing: contributing, being an integral part of the team and the effort. Am I doing the right thing It's about moral courage and integrity."

"Certainly, where I have worked, the wonderful BUZZ of doing something well and together instills hope that it is worth it, and it usually is."

"I have self-worth. I can effect change and value to the organization."

TYPES OF WORTH

Our respondents had much to say about worth as a principle of hope. As a way to make sense of what we heard, we categorized the sum and substance of their comments according to these two questions: Was it mostly about them as individuals or about others? Was their frame mostly immediate or was it deeper and more lasting? This resulted in a four-pane "Window of Worth," as seen in the following chart.

We offer the suggestion that there is a natural sequence in how this important principle of hope is or can be developed. Our respondents appeared more likely to be motivated by noble pursuits when they were assured in their hope for local needs and humble aspirations. Savvy human resource managers anticipate a "WIIFM?" question (**What's In It For Me?**—the acronym pronounced "wif-um") underlying individual concerns at work—it turns out that WIIFM? is a point of entry to a hopeful place.

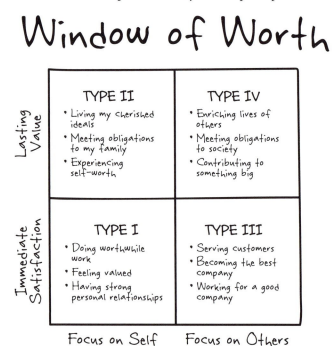

Window of Worth

	Focus on Self	**Focus on Others**
Lasting Value	**TYPE II** • Living my cherished ideals • Meeting obligations to my family • Experiencing self-worth	**TYPE IV** • Enriching lives of others • Meeting obligations to society • Contributing to something big
Immediate Satisfaction	**TYPE I** • Doing worthwhile work • Feeling valued • Having strong personal relationships	**TYPE III** • Serving customers • Becoming the best company • Working for a good company

Type I Worth: "What's In It For Me?"

Type I includes three concerns: First, is the work on my job worth doing? As one respondent said, "People want their work to be worthwhile." Second, do I feel valued? Someone else said, "My contribution is what is important. Does the company value what I bring to the party?" Third, do I enjoy good relationships at work? "Personal relationships at work," according to a third person, "keep you coming back no matter what."

We notice in these three concerns that what people consider to be day-to-day worth includes the sense that there is intrinsic satisfaction in the job itself and in interpersonal connections. Miller and Stiver's comment, though addressed to women, cuts across gender: "We cannot develop a sense of worth unless the people important to us convey that they recognize and acknowledge our experience ... ."[3]

Type II Worth: "What's Really In It For Me?"

As they step out from the perspective of the day to day, people begin talking about "cherished ideals" connected to the heart as well as the mind. Deeper concerns arise, such as having "security with who you are," and "some level of self-worth needed to be willing to hope." "Could I be doing more with my life?" "Can I satisfy myself for now and educate my kids so they will have good lives?" "If I don't feel good about myself it permeates everything I do."

Where in Category I, responsibility falls to the direct supervisor to be involved, there's an opening in Category II for third parties to help. "Coaches, mentors: that's your time to focus on you, your worth."

Type III Worth: "What's In It For My Company?"

When people focus their attention beyond themselves, they think about their place of work. A company's mission, brand, and position in the marketplace can mean a lot. One comment:

> "It pisses me off hearing we're third in some category. That's b.s. I'm not interested in being third in anything. We need to be the best if not the biggest."

This from another person: "I like believing I'm working at a good place. When that's missing, it's hard to get up and come to work."

Type III is also about the added value a company delivers to its customers and clients. "I like touching our consumers' lives much more than just functionally—being there for our consumers, giving them confidence, inspiring them, even a little." Company worth "shows in everything people do: how we interact with vendors, clients, and bosses. We want to contribute to the vision."

Responsibility here lies with the senior management team to create a workplace and culture imbued with meaning and motivation.

Type IV Worth: "What's In It For My Community?"

When people talk about Type IV worth, there is a shift in language. Listen in:

"I'm motivated by enhancing peoples' lives."

"I want to be contributing to something bigger and worthwhile."

"Some tasks are more inherently noble, motivating, but if you have a true customer focus and mindset and use skills that go below the surface, you understand the role your products and services play in a person's life, and you see the value, deliver what matters most."

"The real goal of this company is the driving factor. It makes a difference. Enriching peoples' lives is inspiring."

"It's the value of aspiration, serving people, and overcoming the cynicism regarding marketing. There is a danger of a company having a cause that's very inauthentic, shallow, hollow. It's not about the cause of the day to bring hope in. I'm thinking about a particular biotech organization where I have facilitated strategy conversations. I recall that the thing that people most connected to was 'improving people's lives' through their discoveries."

Type IV worth connects the individual, work group, company, and larger community. Some leaders describe their community in concrete terms as all those who count on the firm for livelihood. Others see community in terms of the human condition. It's a shared responsibility to consider worth on this level, shared by leadership and the stakeholders however defined. Vaclav Havel, leader and poet, made this point in a well known message, in 1986, three years before he became president of Czechoslovakia. When asked, "Do you see a grain of hope anywhere in the 1980s?" Havel replied:

"Hope, in this deep and powerful sense, is not the same as joy that things are going well, or willingness to invest in enterprises that are obviously heading for early success, but, rather, an ability to work for something because it is good, not just because it stands a chance to succeed."[4]

Sequence

There is an order to these events, and three separate people suggested interpretative themes. One said, "Each person needs to assess personal worth and not in relation to others." We would add that each of us is unique in what we hold dear. A second person observed that "it's a circle—the more you start feeling the company has something you feel a part of, the more you start feeling your worth, and the more you help the organization move as a whole." We too see the possibility for virtuous cycles. A third said, "This varies by employee—for some, their whole mission in life is this job, or the job wanted next." We would add that a Type I mission is not less worthy than something in Types II, III, or IV.

We have two cautionary perspectives to shed light on the sequence of things, and one broad conclusion. The conclusion is that the "Window of Worth" offers a valuable view for leaders. Simply put, when all four types of worth are attended to in an organization, there is the potential to provide meaning and motivation for almost everyone. Two "watch-outs" deserve mention, however. A temptation for some leaders is to skip ahead to Type IV worth. A leader whose vision takes in the world but ignores what's in it for individuals or the company, risks being seen as "too idealistic" or "out of touch." There are no short cuts here.

The other warning is that sometimes people are not in great touch with what is most worthwhile or in their own best interests. The standard "workaholic" fits this profile. We would define the problem as over-focus on Type III (basically company needs) and Type I (own immediate concerns) while

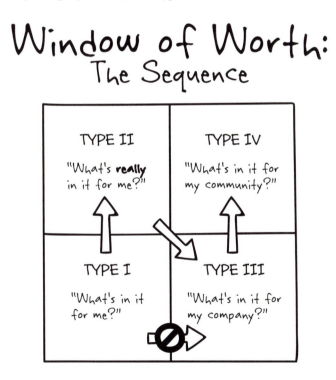

ignoring valid Type II long-term self-interest. The sequence diagram reflects this pattern with a Type II "bypass," moving from Type I directly to III.

SELF-CONCORDANCE

A good way to understand worthy goals is to ask whether they are congruent with the organization's or an individual's value system, and whether they are self-directed and not dictated by others. People are highly motivated by goals that are truly theirs. When "self-concordant" goals are pursued and achieved, they can realize enormous gains in well-being.[5] In the words of several business researchers, "Self-concordance exists when people's goals validly represent their enduring implicit values and interests,"[6] assuming "hoped-for objectives are held to be the best of what is possible, reflecting universal values and often ultimate concerns."[7] Let's look at two instances of self-concordant behavior for the greater good.

Imaginary Lines

Sally Ride, the first American woman in space, is also a physicist on the faculty of the University of California, San Diego. She founded *Sally Ride Science* in 2001 "to empower girls to explore the world of science—from astrobiology to zoology and from environmental engineering to rocket science." Sally Ride's parent company is named Imaginary Lines.

When Harvard President Lawrence Summers spoke to the issue of why women are underrepresented in science and engineering, he suggested innate causality. Three scientists from Stanford University and the Massachusetts Institute of Technology argue that Summers was asking the wrong question. Wondering whether women can excel in math and science was answered long ago by Marie Curie. The right question, they say, is: "How can we encourage more women with exceptional abilities to pursue careers in these fields?" Tapping into the entire talent pool of humanity to make contributions in science and engineering is an imperative, and not just for the United States. "One of the most important and effective actions we can take is to ensure that women have teachers who believe in them and strong, positive mentors, male and female, at every stage of their educational journey—both to affirm and to develop their talents."[8]

As one who benefited from "hopeful" teachers growing up and going through graduate school, Sally Ride is committed to helping girls follow in her path. In her science camps and other events she helps girls "think about themselves" and witnesses the "enthusiasm, spark and sparkle" of fourth and fifth graders getting caught up in science.[9] Her company is concordant with her life.

Lines of Credit

We know a couple of successful former Wall Street bankers who are dedicating their time (one full time, the other part time) to the knotty problem of how to alleviate poverty in the United States. This is a vast challenge with some advances but less progress than would seem achievable. These former bankers are using the training and expertise they acquired on Wall Street to think about the use by and delivery to poor people of financial products most of the nation take for granted, such as paying for all the daily transactions of life. Low-income individuals and families bear higher cost for their financial services either because their transactions are small (by definition) and unit costs (such as fixed charges for using an ATM) are higher relative to the small transaction size or because their lower credit rating induces lenders to charge higher interest rates. Sometimes, services offered by traditional financial providers are not available to low-income families, which permits suppliers of financial services who charge higher prices to fill the unattended demand. Finally, very frequently, the financial literacy of poor people does not allow them to understand fully the cost or other conditions of the financial services they are purchasing. Very often, a higher percentage of the total income of poor people than for middle-income families is taken up by the cost of financial services they purchase; their lack of financial literacy can also result in lost access to funds that are rightfully theirs, such as tax refunds.

For those committed to leveling the playing field for the poor using their understanding of financial systems, their effort is an example of self-concordance. For Jaime Yordan, a former Goldman Sachs partner, with Jim Himes, a former Goldman Sachs colleague, building a company that is aimed at addressing these conditions is an exercise that is "a little step in what I've been doing all my life on Wall Street."

One manager we spoke with never expected to find herself working for a large corporation as a "dirty capitalist." Her self-concordance occurs from the fact that "at least my company has strong values that I agree with."

Charles Handy has pointed out that to associate the purpose of a company with the necessary means to support its continuance is to create a moral muddle. Profit and shareholder return are necessary but not sufficient for worth, and they are not ends in themselves.

History says, Don't Hope
On this side of the grave.
But then, once in a lifetime
The longed-for tidal wave
Of justice can rise up,
And hope and history rhyme.

So hope for a great sea-change
On the far side of revenge.
Believe that a further shore
Is reachable from here.
Believe in miracles
And cures and healing wells.

Seamus Heaney

"The principal purpose of a company is not to make a profit, full stop. It is to make a profit in order to continue to do things or make things, and to do so ever better and more abundantly."[10] Worthy work has positive ends—intrinsic, social, and societal—that attract the means to get there. Capitalism is dirty when profit is the totality of motive.

Elsewhere Handy quotes the visionary businessman David Packard in answer to the question, "Why are we here?"

> "I think many people assume, wrongly, that a company exists solely to make money. Money is an important part of a company's existence, if the company is any good. But the result is not a cause. We have to go deeper and find the real reason for our being ... a group of people get together and exist as a company, so they are able to accomplish something collectively that they could not accomplish separately—they make a contribution to society ... ."[11]

MAKING A DIFFERENCE

The principle of worth establishes that worthy purposes provide meaning and motivation. Meaningfulness resides in the space between the trivial and the grandiose. Short-term goals are trivial if unconnected to larger aims. The likely response is to see them as silly. At the other end, trying to be biggest and best in everything is grandiose, and the normal reaction is to dismiss the effort altogether. When an organization sets goals for itself that are not in its own best interests, people know it, and it's hard for them to be inspired.

When goals are disconnected from peoples' lives and not made relevant to their personal concerns, it's hard for them to care much beyond their paychecks. Nor is there much use in going to the other extreme. When people feel as if everything they say or do is loaded with content, they're likely to feel first overwhelmed and then unmotivated. Hope's objects must be worthwhile for us to feel energy and purpose.

The principle of worth at work extends beyond those making an obvious contribution to society—nurses, firemen, musicians, teachers, and so on. People can find meaning and a sense of calling no matter what their work. We can find it by loving our intrinsic labors. We can find it by delivering products and services that make us proud. We can find it by shaping our jobs to have personal significance. And we can find it in the integrity of our organizational cultures, colleagues, and leaders when they live by values that mirror our own. Hope inspired by worth reminds us of our best selves.

We are in sharp agreement with Barry Schwartz's warning that positive psychology must be able to tell people what a meaningful and good human life entails; to use his term, hope must be "contentful."[12] He means there must be substance to hope—you can't change the world by changing how you think about it. And we are in sharp disagreement with hope theorists who argue for value-neutrality when it comes to goals. Hope presumes human betterment and is never served by self-dealing leaders, conflicts of interest, anticompetitive business strategies, imperious relationships with suppliers, arbitrary interpersonal behaviors, or neglected environmental custodianship. Simply put, hoping never violates the golden rule or bankrupts the commonweal.

So what is truly worthwhile? Can we envision a workplace where all of us want to show up, everyday, ready to rock and roll? Where we willingly offer ourselves without keeping score? Where we achieve sustaining results admirably?

"I want to make a difference," we were told in an interview by one person who really spoke for many. "Hope is profound—worth is a precondition."

Chapter 8

Openness

Hoping does not mean to have *a number of hopes at one's disposal. It means, rather, hoping to* be *open.*[1]

Jurgen Moltmann

Several years ago, Procter & Gamble's (P&G) beauty care business had an awakening. Built on mainstream brands such as Cover Girl and Max Factor, P&G had largely neglected the needs of ethnic women. Meanwhile, competing companies were beginning to grasp the fact that minorities, now the fastest growing component of the U.S. population, are the majorities of tomorrow.

A small team within the beauty business of P&G set out to make a difference. They realized that the beauty category is uniquely sensitive to differences in ethnicity—think of skin tones, color, and product preferences. Their goal was to go beyond the company's superficial points of connection with the ethnic market (such as providing culture-specific models in advertising) and develop a line of products dedicated to the ethnic consumer. So they set out to ground themselves in African-American, Chinese-American, and Mexican-American cultures to understand women's attitudes toward beauty and to define their beauty care needs. By personally immersing themselves in the ethnic woman's world, her home, neighborhood, and stores, the team would gain deep, personal understanding and empathy. They quoted in their presentations the words of former P&G CEO, John Pepper:

"Let us never forget that we are in the business to improve the lives of our consumers.... This means we must think like consumers; put ourselves in their shoes.... Doing this requires that we go beyond understanding consumers. We must respect them and have affection for them as individuals."

In designing the project, one of the team's most important epiphanies was the realization that in order to be open to what was "out there," they had to begin by being open to what was "in here." That meant confronting their own stereotypes and cultural biases. To do that they created a diverse team that represented multiple aspects of the business and mirrored the three ethnic groups they were studying: a Chinese-American product developer, an African-American marketer, and a Mexican-American ad agency representative. Partnered with Caucasian teammates, they brought the voice of their own experience into the room and served as cultural guides for the fieldwork.

To get started, the team, working with an anthropologist, took a hard look at their personal and cultural biases and beliefs. They established a high degree of safety and openness with one another and talked about ethnicity for the first time in a work setting that was not related to a diversity training program. Their goal was to begin the fieldwork with open eyes and minds, what Harvard Psychologist Ellen Langer would call "a mindful state" where thinking is open to creating new categories.

Each team of two visited a minority woman in her home twice. The African-American team member and her partner were in Atlanta, the Chinese American and her partner in San Francisco, and the Mexican American and his partner in Los Angeles. Additionally, the whole team immersed itself in the cultural milieu of the three cities.

The experience formed lasting impressions. In Atlanta, they visited the Martin Luther King historic site and were moved by what they learned about the Civil Rights struggle. When they went to an upscale restaurant they found themselves to be both underdressed and the only white people there. In San Francisco, they visited the Chinese Cultural Center, which documents the struggles of the early immigrants, and they walked the back streets of Chinatown. There they stumbled into a cookie factory staffed by grandmotherly types who specialized in X-rated fortunes. In Los Angeles they toured diverse neighborhoods. At a swap meet they attracted the unwelcome scrutiny of security guards. They were walking in other people's shoes.

The team learned much about their brands that was relevant to marketing and product development and much that was relevant personally. Here is how one person described it:

> *Hope is born while facing the unknown and discovering that one is not alone*
>
> Andre Lacocque and Pierre-Emmanuel Lacocque

"We all felt that we were changed by this experience. We all came back feeling we had learned something, but more importantly, became a part of something.

Or perhaps something became a part of us? We have enormous energy to represent these groups to our business partners."

Inspired, the team chose to do something very unusual in a corporate context. When they made their final presentation to the company, they related their personal journey—a story of openness, hope, and courage:

> "The Ethnic Learning Expedition was formed. The team that came together was enthusiastic about the project because it was the RIGHT thing to do. I was excited to be part of the team and ready to discover more about these people. I had never done anything like this before—going right into people's homes and their lives.

> "I really didn't know much about these people . . . . I was uncomfortable because I didn't know very much and a little anxious about how I would be received in their homes. Would I intrude on their lives? Would I be respectful or accidentally disrespectful? How would I be treated? Would they isolate me or even speak to me on a personal level because I'm different than they are?

> "To prepare for this adventure, I explored my own perceptions and biases about [this] group and identified them. I wanted to make myself aware by opening my mind and heart. I wanted to see and hear what they experience. I wanted to walk in their shoes and peek into their lives.

> "So off I went with my tape recorder and camera to explore their homes, their neighborhoods, and their lives. I immersed myself in their worlds.

> "And then, something unexpected started to happen. Suddenly, as I stood there in the homes, on the streets, and in the world's of these people, I became them. I felt what it was like to be them . . . .

> "I realized how disconnected I was from the way they live their lives. How little I or anyone really knew about these people. BUT YOU KNOW WHAT? They weren't so [strange] after all . . . . We connected on a human level that made all these differences seem trivial. I felt a kinship with them that changed my perceptions I had so carefully listed when I started my journey."

OPENING INWARD, OPENING OUT

"Open" is the ancestor of "up," as in raising a lid or cover, and the word "openness" means not being shut, confined, or sealed. It implies vulnerability, receptivity, accessibility, and freedom from prejudices. Openness warrants new questions and surprising answers. Hope thrives in an environment that applauds innovative ideas and authorizes challenges to biases. Hope celebrates uncertainty.

The P&G story of ethnographic research in beauty care teaches how hope can accrue on several levels at once. Obviously there is a desire on the part of the company and its managers to enter a profitable new market. Good new products will satisfy particular customers, creativity will be rewarded in pursuit of those new products, and cross-cultural sensitivity will be acknowledged for its role in directing creativity. Careers will be assisted and perhaps lives will be changed. Listen to how the speaker quoted above concludes:

> "I felt a sense of shame because our job is to improve the lives of the world's consumers, yet not everything we do is in the best interests of these people that I came to know.
>
> "I want to make a difference but I'm afraid. Am I now the minority in a culture that doesn't have the same understanding that I now do? Am I alone in my desire to improve their lives? Do *we* have the courage to make a difference?"

So, on a deeper level being open to what was "in here" as well as what was "out there" worked a certain magic. The unexpected happened, and the process unfolded in a way that wasn't conscious or linear. Whether we say openness invites the spirit of discovery or just that "luck happens," there are practical implications for this principle of hope. Let's explore the two factors of openness as we understand them—unexpected ends and paradoxical means—and link them back to the daily practices of leadership.

UNEXPECTED ENDS

The principle of openness holds the world as a place of unrealized potential, where discoveries and strokes of genius gestate. Hope lives in an open system of reality where we welcome what we envision but can't predict. For Ernst Bloch, the German philosopher who wrote *The Principle of Hope*, a far-reaching cultural critique of more than a thousand pages, the primary motivating forces for people are "dreams of a better life." Although Bloch's philosophy of hope and the future is socialist at its core, it draws from a humanist anthropology that would be right at home with a capitalist study of beauty care. Bloch sees "utopian content" everywhere he looks, not only in the great works of high culture but in everyday experience—including grooming and fashion, through which we demonstrate to others our potential of being something better. Advertising, novels, films, and television—every human activity, he argues—contain seeds of hope for a positive future.[2]

Bloch's philosophy of hope is echoed in statements made by our respondents. Here are three:

> "I love it when things are uncharted, when I don't see barriers and everything is a step forward. Instead of bucking the existing system, it allows for creativity, endless possibilities and flexibility."

> "There are so many people closed down, but when you find the door handle you can stay open, get rid of being judgmental, endure the chaos, build on others' ideas, and go with the flow."

> "I believe one of the skills that helps nurture hope is that of acceptance of where we are. As students (of life or anything else), we will want to give up numerous times during our journey of study. Especially when we feel we have failed or are making no obvious progress. We must learn to accept where we really are and be willing to 'not know' the outcome. This skill actually paves the way for another flavor of hopefulness which includes not knowing the future but somehow trusting that it will be good and right for us. This is where hope and faith and trust seem to intersect and weave together to form a formidable positive outlook."

The research psychologist C. Rick Snyder and his team write that a "socially hopeful atmosphere" can open the exploration of human talents. Organizational hopefulness fosters discovery, exploration and potentially "changing the game."[3] If "game-changers" are what we want—these could be breakthroughs in innovation or quality, for example, we first need to listen to what our respondents said about telling the truth without fear of reprisal.

Truth and Transparency

The people we interviewed could not be clearer about how much the truth matters. When there is truth and transparency at work, unexpected and welcome outcomes are more likely to occur. Honesty encourages positive surprises because credit will go where deserved. Here are some unvarnished statements—note the plain language and straightforward messages:

> "You can't inspire hope if you're viewed as someone who is not saying the truth."

> "Transparency is the key to hope."

> "I'm most hopeful at work when the environment is transparent and open."

> "When there's truth looking forward, I'm more willing to expose more and say more."

"It's very de-motivating to be pressured to tell people what they want to hear."

"Hope takes risk and courage and gives back both."

"The leader's willingness to speak the truth is matched with my willingness to engage."

According to another respondent, here's what it is like when things get tight—note the jumble of images:

"The effect of stress is that people get almost frozen; they get over-whelmed in trying to deflect what's coming at them. They can't let up for a second or the avalanche gets them. Hope means action, but they don't think they can take action. They're sucked down into a hole. They lose openness. They come out of the chute and keep going. The pace of life hooks you to keep responding. To function like that, hope goes away."

And here's the net result: "There's no room for expansiveness and creativity." The contrast with what this leader is accomplishing is striking:

"Here there is a very unveiled atmosphere. It's the least political company I've worked in. The GM knows everyone by first name. It feels like if you don't tell the truth you're discrediting being the best."

For us the relationship to unexpected positive ends is syllogistic: no truth, no transparency, no sweet surprises.

Freedom and Fear

In our interviews about hope, we were told how fear blocks truth and transparency. People can be "afraid to let others see what they don't know," or fearful of being misunderstood and held lacking "purity of intention," or scared of the consequences of "speaking up for the right thing." Here is a leader describing how relative freedom can replace fear:

"We take risks and look for new paths to get this organization more open to the changing marketplace and changing business model. It doesn't come naturally to get out of our comfort zone. It can be very threatening to others, but to me it's exciting. I will push then see when to back off. People go through different stages before becoming more comfortable. It's going a little slower then I'd like, but we'll ultimately get there."

In a context of hope, people talk about how "closed minds never experience possibility," how "controlling" prevents "leaps of faith," and vividly, about how "the shackles" need to be cut off in order to "come with new ideas or challenge the prevailing thought of day."

Two specific ideas for leaders were advanced. For one, recognizing that bad news travels faster than good, consider "full amnesty" if people are open. Reward messengers and attack problems, not people. For another, make it common practice to identify the "elephant in the room" or "the moose on the table"—whatever exists in common awareness but is taboo to talk about. Sanction the freedom to challenge myths and explore the validity of "hallway wisdom."

Quality and Innovation

Quality processes, paradoxically, can be opposed to openness in organizations.[4] To the extent that quality means taking variation out of systems and processes, it reduces deviation—both positive and negative. Thus, an unplanned piece of good news or a surprising win can create as much scurrying about as an expected failure. Being outside "control limits," even on the high side, can indicate a process failure. Organizational cultures in their very fabric work toward equilibrium, meaning they routinely edit wild ideas and castigate mavericks. When control-chart mentality is applied indiscriminately, consistency trumps diversity. Hopeful openness on the other hand is essentially inclusive of people, ideas, and outcomes. We were told:

"Openness invites discovery and people connecting to it."

"If you are open, you are open for hope to come from anywhere."

"Hope sparks discovery."

The principle of openness is critical to innovation. Innovation literally means "the ability to begin or introduce something new, to be creative." It is a hopeful act in and of itself, an act of becoming and believing in the future.

In thriving organizational cultures, the process of innovation extends beyond new product or business development to all functions. It is considered the lifeblood of tomorrow, the only way to keep pace with change. Yet when promising new ideas fly in the face of today's mental models or take us outside our comfort zones, forward-looking leadership is required. Innovation begins with a leader's commitment to openness—to keen ears and fresh eyes, affirming minds and caring hearts.

PARADOXICAL MEANS

In 1994, Charles Handy wrote that "there is paradox at the heart of things" and extended that basic notion into a prescient guide to leadership in an age of increasing turbulence.[5] There is the paradox of teamwork, for example. What is the relationship between individuality and collective effort? There is no "I" in the word team, yet as Michael Jordan has pointed out, there is indeed an "I" in the word WIN! For Handy, paradoxes contain unexpected twists and simultaneous opposites, not to be resolved but managed, which is a paradox in itself. Handy could have been writing about hope.

Leadership Behavior

In *Good to Great*, Jim Collins tells the remarkable story of Admiral Jim Stockdale, who was captured, imprisoned, and tortured in North Vietnam for eight years. Stockdale did more than survive—he exercised his command and resisted his captors in creative, courageous ways. When Collins asked Stockdale who among his fellow prisoners didn't survive the ordeal, he answered that it was the optimists—those whose faith wasn't built on realistic appraisal of the circumstances. Collins describes this lesson as the "Stockdale Paradox": "Retain faith that you will prevail in the end, regardless of the difficulties. AND at the same time confront the most brutal facts of your current reality, whatever they might be."[6]

Though less dramatic, our respondents described leadership paradoxes of their own. Here is what might be called the "vulnerability paradox" described in different ways:

"I know about the willingness to confront reality and be vulnerable in the process. When leaders are vulnerable, expressing their humanity creates a connection between the leader and the organization."

"I'm respectful of others and their ideas. Assuming positive intent, making the charitable assumption, you're really open to possibility. But it's a fine balance of being open to outcome and needing to make a decision."

Here is the "openness paradox"

"This is tricky. When you're an executive and see bad times ahead, you have to be careful how you communicate and still keep hope alive. How much do you communicate? When and how? We tell the truth, but maybe not until asked, and then we tell the truth with optimism based on our experience and beliefs."

"I'm an open book, and I have an open door policy. I always give benefit of the doubt first. Sometimes it's painful to be open. I'm not naïve, but I do get burned."

"To be nurtured, the human spirit needs to be open and ready. Some people have been so hurt that they will protect themselves by not allowing themselves to hope so as not to be hurt again. There needs to be courage to face what may come, the good and the difficult. Hope needs to be recognized and supported in one another."

"I try to be open so people can come to me, talk to me. Hierarchy makes me almost angry—they distrust my intention because of my position. It's not about me."

Another was explicit about the "paradox of control":

"I do not hope that a situation I am in will necessarily change … my 'true' hope lies in knowing that the reason I am in the difficult situation is one that I may not yet be aware of… . In other words I surrender… . There is a very close linkage of *hope* and *surrender*. Most people would agree that the two words are interrelated but in a different way than I do. It is a common belief that when you give up hope, it is time to surrender. I believe that you surrender *because* you have hope. You surrender to the life you are given, you surrender to the present moment, you surrender to a universal plan that you are unaware of, knowing and trusting that all things are working together for your highest good at all times."

> *Now hope that is seen is not hope. For who hopes for what he sees? But if we have hope for what we do not see, we wait for it with patience.*
>
> *Romans 8:12*

As ways to "manage" paradoxes of leadership, there were these suggestions:

"Be open to admitting what you don't know and to new approaches."

"Welcome collective discovery."

"Show your feelings and thinking as a leader."

"Be willing to visualize the future outside existing paradigms."

"Know your filters, paradigms and frames of reference."

"Moderate your attitude by self-awareness."

Here is how one leader talks about working the process:

"I watch body language. I have certain people who are my bellwethers. I know who has a lot of capacity, and I feel and watch their stress. Sometimes I have no choice, but often I do: I can back off, or I can jump in and surround them with support."

Finally, there are multiple paradoxes associated with success and failure, as sometimes it is not so easy to distinguish success and failures, or indeed it takes failure to reach success. Therefore the following anecdote makes sense: "One manager, just promoted, has worked on every failure."

Meeting Management

The organizational world is characterized by meetings, conferences, and group activities. Even though meetings are increasingly "virtual" (electronically enabled), there are still too many for most of us. In our efforts to make the best use of our time in these gatherings, our impulse is to impose the formal structures of agendas, defined roles, and agreed outcomes. Yet a complete prescription for meeting effectiveness must include the paradoxical provision for the unexpected to happen within time held open.

Try this as a thought experiment: Remember the best meetings you have ever attended and consider the elements that made them effective. Were they timely? Well led? Efficient? Organized? Respectful? Prepared for in advance? Perhaps all of these characteristics were present. Now think about the outcomes of those best meetings. How did they come about? Possible answer: a positive breakthrough occurred in the group's collective understanding or relationship in a moment of openness. You saw something together, felt something, or agreed to do something. That moment of group-mindedness wasn't on the agenda.

Jon Katzenbach's influential study of leadership teams concludes with guidelines for all levels of teams; the final one is, "Set aside open-ended times for working together." Tightly structured meetings have their place, yet "the tighter the agenda and schedule, the less likely real work can occur."[7] Applying the principle of openness to goal-setting suggests finding minimum critical specifications for performance. Overdetermined specifications limit possibilities. Underdetermined or absent specifications yield incoherence. Hopeful practice lies in the paradoxical middle ground.

SPIRITUAL ELBOWROOM

As a principle of hope, openness provides the context for the other four. Hope is both principled and paradoxical, and openness holds the balance. Openness is held back by our perfectionism—the urge to tidy things up and make them presentable, predictable, and prescribed. On the other hand, openness is stretched too thin when there are no boundaries whatsoever. Openness requires both trust and risk. Neither of the following two images can capture the paradox of trust and risk. The circle represents perfection, and the circle with arrows represents unbounded energy. Neither shows the openness required by hope.

Perhaps a more adequate symbol to exemplify openness is a version of the vesica pisces, on the right, a symbol for life—this one is a crop circle observed at Tegdown Hill, Patcham, East Sussex, UK. Ancient patterns and forms such as these can help us visualize the essential mystery of hope.

Perfection   Unbounded Energy   Openness

Neither the perfect nor the unbounded encourage hopeful openness.

Should leaders welcome the unknown? Obviously yes, but how? Too much openness and guidance is without form or function. Too little and hope is reduced to rigid inflexibility. We were told that "risk and courage evoke fear—and sacredness. What is implied is boundless, not the safety of being prescriptive."

Hope is inspired by listening to the call of the human spirit for elbowroom. In our experience, when the *how* of achieving goals is open to the resourcefulness of the achievers, we're not surprised when goals are met or exceeded, or when there are remarkable discoveries. Hope exists in the willingness to expect the unexpected and wrestle with ambiguity on the road to self-knowledge.

Chapter 9

Connection

Hope is something we do with others. Hope is too important—its effects on body and soul too significant—to be left to individuals alone. Hope must be the responsibility of the community.[1]

Kathy Weingarten

Our most cherished hopes are pointless outside community. We know from experience that we can only make really important things happen *in* relationship with others. We know too that really important things are *about* relationship with others. And on a deeper level we sense that what we relate *to* is the call of the future.

The principle of connection harmonizes hope's principles. In hopeful connection people are grounded in who they are, they know where they've come from, and they're striving to get where they've chosen to go together.

TWO CASES OF CONNECTION

"Business is all relational," we were told, and "shared hope is mutually energizing." Social science is on the same page. A comprehensive review of the literature reached the conclusion that hope is fundamentally relational—always connected to relationship.[2] C.R. Snyder and his colleagues at the University of Kansas reports that in study after study, when people who test as having higher hope are compared with others, hope is highly correlated with satisfaction in interpersonal relations.[3] Robert Putnam draws on employee surveys of job satisfaction to conclude that social connections at work may be the strongest predictor of job satisfaction.[4] We have two stories to tell about how the principle of connection works at work—note how in both situations people connect to each other in authentic ways and, just as important, to accurate appraisals of real conditions.

Healthcare Connection

Thedacare is a community health system in Northern Wisconsin consisting of three hospitals as well as clinics, physicians' services, laboratories, and senior care facilities. It's the largest employer in the state's second largest economic market. It's also the winner of multiple awards based on consumer perceptions of quality and is a leader in healthcare improvement.

John Toussaint, MD, is CEO and leader of a quality improvement process within Thedacare that was borrowed from, of all places, the Toyota Motor Corporation. All car companies and many other manufacturers have been learning from Toyota for the past decade, as the "Toyota Production System" has become the gold standard. Toyota invented a system known as Lean production in the 1950s that speeds up processes, reduces waste, and improves quality. Toussaint is in the forefront of applying Lean to healthcare.

"Lean is the potential salvation of healthcare," he predicts. "In ten years this will be how everything is done." For Toussaint, "this is about hope."

> "We want a system where people don't make mistakes—that's where people want to work. Are nurses and doctors happy when they make mistakes? The system itself causes mistakes. The idea of mistake-free healthcare is an exciting vision.

> "I was getting burned out—my job was all 'slash-and-burn' to cut costs. This new process has given us some hope. We're meeting our financial targets without slash-and-burn, and our quality performance measures are in the 95th percentile nationwide."

Let's look under the hood. First, most of the fourteen principles of the "Toyota Way" in Lean manufacturing techniques can be tailored to any enterprise that produces outcomes. The first Toyota Way principle is the starting point: "Base your management decisions on long-term philosophy, even at the expense of short-term financial goals."[5] This includes having a sense of purpose, bigger than making money, to generate value for society while acting with both self-reliance and trust—ideas perfectly compatible with healthcare.

Steven Spear, a senior fellow at the Institute for Healthcare Improvement, in an article titled "The Health Factory," writes that hospitals can indeed learn from companies such as Toyota, Vanguard, and Alcoa. These and other nonhealthcare improvement leaders are constantly learning how to do work better and then sharing knowledge "through collaborative experimentation in which all employees take part."[6]

Roger Gerard, Ph.D., Chief Learning Officer at Thedacare, explains how they've been able to develop and launch their Thedacare Improvement System—notice how thoroughly they employ the principle of connection along their journey. After spending years in traditional quality programs and achieving modest returns, according to Gerard, they stumbled across Lean at a conference in 2002 and said "this is the one." With some outside help, they began to hold week-long improvement meetings including all the associates in a given area where there was an opportunity to make positive changes. The process quickly paid for itself, and now there are twenty-five of these events being held each month, led by twenty-five of Thedacare's best associates. John Toussaint reviews progress with these teams every Friday morning.

To keep everyone involved, "structured conversations" occur at all levels of the organization and in many configurations. There are designed and scheduled one-on-one meetings, town hall sessions, and informal conversations in the training room. A requirement of their educators is that they embed every clinical and nonclinical course with a sense of Thedacare's mission, vision, and values. One of their core values is to show respect for other people whether or not they are present—it's "distasteful" at Thedacare to talk disparagingly of people behind their backs. "Hope is a function of relationships," says Gerard.

Then there are the annual company "Follies." Dozens of associates work for weeks with a professional director to prepare skits, routines, and musical performances—John Toussaint plays the trumpet—and the whole town is invited to see the show. It's held at the new community arts center, and the place fills up. In Gerard's words, it's a demonstration of "people in the community being human and loving one another."

Finally, it's revealing to note that Thedacare is intentionally trying to reduce their internal use of the word "organization" and replace it with the word "community."

The Fair Trade Connection

Equal Exchange is "a worker cooperative dedicated to Fair Trade" located in West Bridgewater, Massachusetts. Worker owned co-ops are part of an alternative economy whereby employees own the company on a one-person/one-share/one-vote basis, share equally in profits or losses, elect their own boards of directors from within their ranks, and govern themselves by transparent, democratic principles. In this model everyone is held to the same rules, and held accountable by others within the co-op.

Rodney North, who is an inside Board Director of Equal Exchange, began his career as a "pick and shovel" man in archeology, but he wanted to do more to change the world. He later spent time in Guatemala, volunteered there in an orphanage, and studied international economics, focusing on Latin America. Along the way he began to question the presumption of those around him that business was necessarily "part of the problem" and could never be "part of the solution" for the developing world. He reasoned that if commerce is indeed the most powerful and dynamic part of the economy, maybe it could be converted to something more sustainable, more "hopeful and helpful," in his words. His hope was to infect business with Peace Corps-type ideals.

> *My hope is the spirit of family and community where the center of my being is never left without help, rooted in culture and sacred order.*
>
> *High Eagle, Sioux founder of a home for children*

Now more advocates of an alternative economy are seeing "business" as more of an opportunity than an obstacle. While the media has abbreviated and simplified globalization, North sees the opportunity for a "grassroots globalization" that benefits all. The business world, for him, is not a monolith but a "crowd with many voices." His message is, "you don't have to wrestle with large corporations—you can create your own enterprises, build on solutions, and encourage the market to follow." North says,

> "Hope is the fuel for building something—something better, and is different from the fear that often feeds the resistance to Nike, The Gap, or the WTO. Hope is about creating something, not stopping something. Hope is pragmatic."

Equal Exchange is like a group of gardeners who "don't confuse themselves with their tulips." Their co-op is not just about coffee or chocolate bars. The basic idea is to trade in an economy of fairness, where "hope may be the greatest benefit we have to offer small farmers." To that end, co-op members are connected in both their livelihood and their vision. Thus they "invest disproportionately" in their hiring processes, paying a lot of attention to "getting the right people on the bus." Their Fair Trade worker co-op is not a "utopia" according to North, but "to have work that we feel better about is a bargain—even if the trade-off might mean a smaller house and an older car." For Equal Exchange, "hope is not free, easy, a frill, or irrelevant."

THE SEVEN C'S OF CONNECTION

When we engaged people in conversations about hopeful connection in the context of their jobs, their careers and their vocations, we heard about multiple connecting *points*. As you will see, the primary ways people feel connected at work extend well beyond what is normally measured in job satisfaction surveys. We categorized responses and arranged them from the most personal to the most universal. These seven ways people connect to work underlie every organizational conversation, no matter what. Hopeful leaders find ways to connect where they want people to go with where people are and what they really want.

Core

Connection is "core to the human experience" said one manager, and the "core of humanity" said another. This is what is core to five others:

"You can't be hopeful by yourself. You're most hopeful in relationship."

"You don't realize your worth without others."

"I'm open to connection—discovering something new about myself and others and gaining an enhanced sense of self-worth."

"The challenge for me is not allowing someone else to define success for me and staying spiritually grounded. I don't want to be living someone else's dream."

"Hope has both elements, the individual and the collective, and it's relationship-based. An individual can influence her own world to some extent, but you still need to be relational. No man is an island. Success requires both."

So, "You can't feel hope if you're isolated." And, "Everyone has something to contribute. I can't imagine hope without connection."

Colleagues

People feel connected to their colleagues, their teams, their networks, and their "communities of practice."

"To truly succeed here is to have the ability genuinely to connect with people—with care, understanding, and empathy—then to inspire and support. Share paths they might not see or might feel intimidated by. Allow people to experience their strengths and capabilities."

"I have global colleagues . . . . Hope is driven by the relationships you have. You want to rely on your colleagues, enjoy success together, see each other grow and develop. Sometimes you challenge and provoke, and other times celebrate."

"People create ideas. Teams create innovation. You won't succeed without the collaborative element."

"Working with colleagues allowed us to think in more complex ways and make connections to different aspects of our thoughts. It was exciting. The sum is greater than the parts."

"Innovation is about different ideas and the ability to connect different relationships with more exposed diverse points of view."

This is definitely not "faux connection," where "you think you're connecting but you're playing a game with nods, listening but taking no action, and being two-faced." Connection at work means you're working with genuine allies, where there is both substantial shared trust as well as agreement.

Company

Respondents told us how they wanted to "breathe more emotional life into the corporation" and create authentic connections to their organizations. Not this:

"If your idea is not well received and you are discounted, shamed, you start telling the organization what it wants to hear and it creates an inauthentic connection. You as a person are not engaged in the outcome. You took a risk. The lesson taught is shut down. Next time, there's a smaller voice, and you're less of a person—until you stop trying altogether."

For too many of us, the workplace is our community. Jay Zimmerman, Chairman of the Bingham McCutchen law firm, acknowledges, "A properly constructed workplace can be an enormously supportive system for people—a real grounding."

Customers

For some, there is a primary connection to their "relationships with each other and customers."

"It's constant work in progress making sure you're spending time in the right way connecting to the customer and each other. You have to be willing to work at those relationships. The world pulls us into 'doing' so it's easy to get lost."

"It's a blurry line: are we working for ourselves or for the customer? It's not about the distinction between taking care of self versus taking care of customer. Customer intuitively knows it's there. The finer points connect us all."

One theme that surfaced repeatedly was the importance of having a direct line of sight to the customer:

"Seeing how the company's goal of improving our customers' lives plays through to the end user. That emotional connection feeds me as well as her."

Then there is this comment from a therapist: "Hope comes from an understanding of where your client is."

Community

Whether community is defined as the neighborhood or the globe, "community makes hope more possible, and vice versa."

"Beyond the workplace and in every aspect of your life, it's amazing how easy it is to learn through connection because of its stimulating effect. If you connect, you learn a lot—expressing hope is connecting—and you find common ideals that bind us together as a community."

For some, there is a common thread in "how I connect with overall goals, other people, the workplace, and the community."

Common Ground

Connecting to common ground means meeting each other in a shared place of values and ideas, where we're "not alone, talking and listening, and we're getting hope from each other."

"There's a win-win. There's common ground. Agreement is not necessary. We can disagree yet understand."

"When I was in the Peace Corps, I think we all had hope of making the country and village we served a better place. Even in the face of huge obstacles such as corruption and disease, we felt we could make a difference. Why did we feel this way? I think we had a sense of mission and purpose."

"Connections are made clearer by strategy and mission—things you can rally around and get emotional and passionate about. They fuel a common language. Growing a brand by 7% is just not energizing."

For one manager the conversation about company vision, mission, and tactics "made me step back... . Where does hope fit?"

Cosmos

People value "being part of something; people don't leave companies for money." Connection to this larger something is "connecting the dots to human, temporal and mental dimensions."

"For me, hope is nurtured by the recognition that I am part of something larger in the cosmos. It's quite literally 'Not (just) about Me.' This makes the hard times less personal and the good times even more of a gift."

"There's 'uber' hope and mini-hopes. I've been starting to talk more about breaking things down. Hope isn't just a dream. The bigger picture is inspiring but can be overwhelming. Can there be a mini in a larger? Because at the end of the day we all want to feel connected. Our stories yearn to come together into a collective version."

"With fast growth, the danger is losing connection through the press of business, the number of meetings. I yearn for time and space to sit back and make connections with ideas."

Finally, there is connection with the future: "Hope connects here and now and future possibility."

THE PRACTICE OF CONNECTION

The Seven C's of Connection lend themselves to a set of questions about how things are today in an organization, and how people want things to be. The following chart demonstrates in a simple way what a leadership team might want to know. The examples in the cells are all positive, yet there is always room to create more and different ways to build connection. Asking honestly, "Do we have empathy?" and, "Are we on solid ground?" will engage the power of hope. Even more, by affirming seven or more forms of connection that go beyond those between profits and paychecks, a leadership team will engage heads, hearts, and hands.

CONNECTION ➡	TO PEOPLE Do we have empathy?	TO REALITY Are we on solid ground?	KEEP/CHANGE/CREATE What do we recommend?
CORE	We build on individual strengths	Rewards recognize different contributions	
COLLEAGUES	Our teams share ideas and resources	Our overhead costs are low	
COMPANY	It's a good place to work	It's easy to recruit good people	
CUSTOMERS	We know our customers well and they know us	Our customers are loyal	
COMMUNITY	We're a good corporate citizen	We go beyond what the law requires	
COMMON GROUND	We have strong values and ethics	We're highly valued by our stakeholders	
COSMOS	We share a positive vision for the future	We're leaving a legacy	

Two organizational practices that have become second nature to us over the years—practices that enable hopeful connection among associates—are Dialogue and Timeline. Let us describe both.

Dialogue

Performing "real work" in organizations is more than having discussions, making decisions, and delegating responsibilities—real work is akin to *dialogue*, a prime process for building community.

Dialogue is a way of communicating in a group that produces shared meaning by welcoming difference and building a sense of the whole. Its roots are derived from the early Greeks and the council tradition of Native American people. Dialogue is real work because it honors individual perspectives and collective wisdom.

To set the conditions for dialogue, we suggest three simple rules:

1. Listen from the heart—listen to hear not judge, and to affirm not evaluate.
2. Speak the truth of your experience—say what is true for you.
3. Go slowly so more can happen—welcome silence and think in terms of "and" instead of "but."

We employ dialogue on a routine basis whenever there is disconnection. Perhaps an in-group refuses to listen to others, or there is an "undiscussable" topic impeding progress, or the overall purpose of an activity has gotten lost. In one unforgettable dialogue session with the management group of a small business in New Jersey, the "talking stick" (a flip-chart marker was used as the symbolic item) was being passed around the circle with great effect. This was a tough-minded group in a difficult business, and their future was under threat. Yet, "slowing down so more can happen" seemed the obvious thing to be doing. Everyone's views were being heard by everyone else. They talked about everything in human, nonlinear order: their products and customers, how they were treating each other, what was most disappointing and frustrating about how they went about their business, and most important of all, how they felt right there and then, in the moment. One highly technical topic was resistant to logic and analysis, and then suddenly, a solution popped out. Hope was in the air.

Timeline

The practice of storytelling lies at the heart of connection. Storytelling harks back to our most ancient tribal roots. The bonding tales and myths of times gone by, of heroes and their quests told around the campfire, were and are the glue that holds communities together. Our stories connect us to each other and to our shared experiences. Our stories give us identity and meaning. Our stories honor our values and teach our children.

Once we were working with a group of about twenty-five associates at the home base of a company that had, eighteen months before, acquired its primary competitor. We knew there was healing work to do—connecting work—and we thought that telling stories about the past might be a way to do that. We developed an exercise called the Timeline.

The Timeline, by celebrating a community's shared history and life experience, is an awareness activity that builds a foundation for the future. Building a Timeline glorifies the anecdotal and honors individual experience in the context of the whole. We have seen the activity bring out the ghosts of the past to dance—to be acknowledged or, if necessary, busted. Done well, the Timeline gets beneath the tendency to overidealize, reinforces the deeper values of the community, and creates useful, honest perspective on the evolution of the organization.

Imagine a wall covered with mural paper on which is drawn a Timeline representing the greatest number of years of seniority of any member in the room. People arrange themselves along the line in order of seniority and then sign the Timeline at their dates of hire. Next, people cluster into small cohort groups according to when they joined the company, and they are invited to reminisce about what the organization was like when they came aboard. Their task is to come back and tell us about their era—its ups and downs, its themes and headlines. After they transcribe their data to the Timeline using words, pictures, and sticky dots, they tell their stories. We have been privileged to hear anecdotes and tales of adventure that are often hilarious, sometimes quite moving, and always revealing.

In this group from the acquiring and acquired companies, we learned an unforgettable lesson about the importance of connecting past to future and about the healing power of inclusion. Two men from the acquired firm, whose seniority matched anyone's in the room, put themselves on the Timeline—at the year of the acquisition, not the year when they joined the acquired firm. In a moment no one could have predicted, a member of the acquiring company said, "You should put yourselves on the Timeline with all your seniority intact, and tell us about your company over those years before we knew you." They were invited to reclaim twenty-five years of their lives—and their dignity. The moment was profound.

Afterward, a woman told us she was reminded of her son's karate lesson. He had just participated in a ceremony to mark his advancement to the next step. "They throw their belts over their shoulders to symbolize bringing your learning with you as you move forward."

The reason I never give up hope is because everything is so basically hopeless. Hopelessness underscores everything—the deep sadness and fear at the center of life. The holes in the heart of our families, the animal confusion within us; the madness of King George. But when you do give up hope, a lot can happen. When it's not pinned wriggling into a shiny image or expectation, it sometimes floats and opens like one of those fluted Japanese blossoms, flimsy and spastic, bright and warm. This almost always happens in community.

Anne Lamott

ONLY CONNECT!

Disconnected organizations, groups, or relationships can be exclusionary to their great disadvantage. When differences are penalized—whether in race or gender, style or standing, culture or capability—alienation defeats empathy. And at the other extreme, overconnected organizations where everyone seems to be in on everything spawn enmeshed relationships, smother individuality, and violate personal space. Then there is a different kind of disconnection, no less deadly, when organizations drift from the solid ground of reality into the unstable ground of

Hopeful Connection

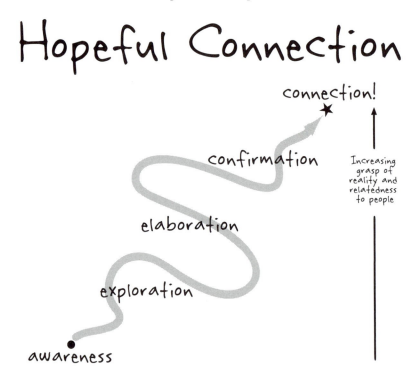

connection!
★

confirmation   Increasing
                            grasp of
                            reality and
                            relatedness
                            to people

elaboration

exploration

●
awareness

fantasy—or when they so greatly exaggerate their problems or opportunities, they run themselves into the ground. In a connected organization people appreciate being joined with each other and with the larger whole, and people are both rooted in reality and drawn to higher callings.

Hopeful connection combines a grasp of reality with relatedness to people, and it proceeds through predictable phases, from the narrow moment of dawning awareness, to more expansive exploration, to fullest elaboration—then, closing back down, from confirmation of choices to pointed, genuine connection.

Hope provides handholds during change, as we grasp reality and relate to each other. "Only connect!" is E.M. Forster's oft-quoted line, so we may "live in fragments no longer."[7]

Chapter 10

The Golden Mean

Hope is a motor not a meter.[1]

Martin Seligman

In May, 2005, when the U.S. Senate was locked in a power struggle over the appointment of judges, a group of about fifteen senators quietly forged a compromise in the middle ground between their Republican and Democratic colleagues. Their work began to shift power away from the extremes in both parties, reviving the political middle. Some lawmakers were optimistic that the moderates could restore comity and across-the-aisle cooperation in the Senate. In politics, it is never sure whether the center will hold. What is clear is that the tenor of work in the Senate shifted, at least for the moment, and the press reported that meetings were "hopeful, businesslike, respectful." According to *The Boston Globe*, "The mere existence of the meetings has aroused hope for a new era in the Senate... ."[2]

Hope resides in the golden mean, the way of reasonableness and wisdom between extremes. Having defined hope as *an orientation to a positive future that engages our heads, hearts and hands,* we've since learned that it acts like one of the moral virtues as defined by Aristotle. Hope appears when its elements hold to a position between excess and deficiency and aims at moderation in thought, feeling, and action. Reassurance that hope has its place in ancient wisdom drives the stark realization that it can be a "hard thing" for a leader to hope. Here is Aristotle in the *Nicomachean Ethics*:

> "And on this account it is a hard thing to be good; for finding the middle or the mean in each case is a hard thing, just as finding the middle or centre of a circle is a thing that is not within the power of everybody, but only of [the person] who has the requisite knowledge.[3]"

So in order to build requisite knowledge needed to put hope to work, we now summarize, distill, and clarify.

PRINCIPLES OF HOPEFUL LEADERSHIP

Let's start by describing hopeful leadership in plain terms and unpack it from there.

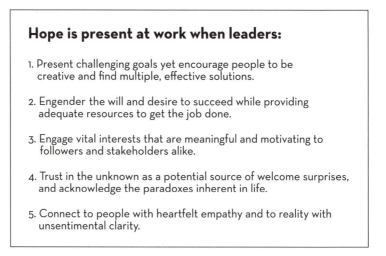

Hope is present at work when leaders:

1. Present challenging goals yet encourage people to be creative and find multiple, effective solutions.

2. Engender the will and desire to succeed while providing adequate resources to get the job done.

3. Engage vital interests that are meaningful and motivating to followers and stakeholders alike.

4. Trust in the unknown as a potential source of welcome surprises, and acknowledge the paradoxes inherent in life.

5. Connect to people with heartfelt empathy and to reality with unsentimental clarity.

Looking through the lens of hope's five principles, we can see why some personal and organizational efforts produce expected results while others don't. We can look at leadership and organizational culture and understand where and how hope can make a positive difference. The following organizational hope scale summarizes the five principles we've introduced in the preceding five chapters. Here's how to read it: The middle column lists the principles with two defining criteria for each. When the criterion (in capital letters) is present, a person may feel what is named in the quotation marks. So, for the principle of possibility when there is a CHALLENGE, one may feel "eager" to meet that challenge. If, however, the challenge is deemed to be an IMPOSSIBILITY, one may well feel "dubious" about it. And if the challenge is no challenge at all, but a SURE THING, then one is likely to feel "superfluous." On the left-hand side, there are indicators beginning with the letter "r"—these are short-hand explanations for the principles. The principle of possibility, for example, is much about "reach": having to reach too far, or not reach at all, defeats hope.

When leaders and their organizations are working between the extremes, the result is additive to hopefulness—a good thing. People feel eager, engaged and empathic toward one another, and so on. When there is deficiency or excess, it's not a good thing. The effect is people feeling ambivalent, annoyed, or alienated, etc. As we recap the five principles, try them on for size and scrutinize your performance as a leader.

HOPE

	Deficiency ○	The Golden Mean ◐	Excess ●

POSSIBILITY

REACH	SURE THING "superfluous"	CHALLENGE "eager"	IMPOSSIBILITY "dubious"
	ONE CHOICE "restricted"	MULTIPLE SOLUTIONS "innovative"	TOO MANY CHOICES "ambivalent"

AGENCY

RESOURCES	UNINVOLVEMENT "apathetic"	ENGAGEMENT "will and desire"	FANATACISM "on guard"
	INSUFFICIENCY "starved"	ADEQUACY "sustained"	OVERABUNDANCE "sloppy"

WORTH

RELEVANCE	TRIVIALITY "disappointed"	MEANING "reassured"	GRANDIOSITY "dismissive"
	LITTLE VALUE "uninvested"	GOOD VALUE "motivated"	INFLATED VALUE "overwhelmed"

OPENNESS

RECEPTIVITY	BLINDESS "confined"	TO THE UNEXPECTED "trusting"	SUSCEPTIBILITY "helpless"
	RIGIDITY "resigned"	TO THE PARADOXICAL "intrigued"	CHAOS "exasperated"

CONNECTION

RELATIONSHIPS	EXCLUSION "alienated"	TO PEOPLE "empathetic"	ENMESHMENT "violated"
	FANTASY "ungrounded"	TO REALITY "solidly grounded"	OPPRESSION "ground down"

Possibility

We hope best when we hope for something in the range of the possible. If we sense that what we can stretch to accomplish what's needed, we feel eager to perform. If our goal seems completely out of reach, we're dubious. And if it is easily within reach, we feel superfluous. Furthermore, when different ways to skin the cat are elicited and affirmed, we feel innovative. If there is only one choice available to us, we feel restricted. When there are too many choices, we feel ambivalent about them all. In the middle range, however, when multiple solutions seem workable, or innovativeness is enacted.

Hope that is deficient or excessive in possibility is *wasted hope*. We waste hope when we dream impossible dreams—it's better just to keep on dreaming. And we waste hope when all we need to do is get off our duff and take care of business—ordinary effort may do the trick. We also waste hope when we restrict ourselves to tried-and-true solutions on one hand, or when we make ill-considered maneuvers on the other. To infer from Aristotle, it's a "hard thing" to get all this right. Nonetheless, it's a core responsibility of leadership.

Agency

We feel a sense of agency when our efforts matter—when we really want to see things through, and we feel our contributions are going to be fruitful. The sense that "I am an agent, an actor, a player" builds self-confidence, and when we follow-through, our positive mood and mode can be sustained.

Too little engagement result in being uninvolved and causes apathy. At the other extreme, fanaticism is when we care too much and lose our balance. Fanatical leaders put us on our guard when we have no sympathy for their causes.

When funds or skills are inadequate, our best efforts may meet predictable fates. We just can't squeeze blood out of stones. Having too much in the kitty is scarcely an improvement—there's nothing like the feeling of sloppiness to slow us down. So agency means it's important to have an appetite and not to be skipping meals.

When agency is either deficient or excessive, it can be *wishful hope*. Lacking agency, we fancifully rely on outside intervention. We prefer to remain passive, and we wish for someone else to take care of things for us. Equally, the overweening sense that "If it's going to be, it's all up to me," is but a wish for that to be so. It turns out that we're rarely at the center of someone else's universe, and no one is indispensable. Wishful leaders put their followers and even themselves at risk of downfall and despair.

Worth

Worth carries the content of hope—it's the moral, ethical, and lasting dimension of what we hope for. When that hoped-for object is genuinely meaningful, we're reassured that our values remain intact and that our moral compass can detect true worth. Furthermore, we're motivated to do the right thing, and we feel engaged.

When a supposed "big deal" is really a trivial matter, however, we're disappointed in our leaders for stooping so low. And when an everyday opportunity is oversold, or an ordinary problem is made to sound like an impending disaster, we turn our attention to the upcoming weekend. Grandiosity turns us off.

Furthermore, pursuits having little real value in our eyes fail to motivate us, as indeed they should, and we resist being invested. In the opposite direction, to make everything momentous, we can be overwhelmed.

When hope's inner virtue is made the calling card for narrowly self-serving purposes, we call that "hijacked hope." Politicians can use hope to get votes (authentically if their constituents resonate with what is hoped for, and cynically if they're spinning the truth). So too can corporations speak of hope to make sales. Here are two recent ads, first from IBM, tapping into hope's power to be positive, and second from AOL selling services by reducing hope to a weak defense against our fears:

IBM announces "ON DEMAND HOPE"

"You can hope you don't get a virus or you can get America Online. America Online provides the protection you need for your whole computer."

By way of comparison, the Red Cross full-page request for funds in the wake of Katrina was compelling on many levels. It illustrated a formula with dramatic images:

−HOME

−ELECTRICITY

−FOOD

+HOPE

At the bottom, there was this simple line: "Hope is more powerful than a hurricane."[4] Everyone speaks of hope, but when leaders speak of hope their credibility is on the line. Their test is always the selfless truth.

Openness

Openness is a characteristic of leaders we love and organizational systems we prefer, though it's not an easy standard to meet. Being truly and authentically open means trusting that what can happen will be beneficial, one way or the other. And when we're faced with life's little conundrums, we're intrigued even when stymied. We know openness best when our sunny outlook toward the unknown is contagious. Blindness to what is going on, however, rather than being awake to what might happen next, causes us to feel confined to the status quo. At the other extreme, being susceptible to the hurly-burly of events leaves us feeling helpless.

When leaders gloss over complexity in an attempt to make everything black and white, their rigidity in the face of paradox leaves us resigned. And when they give equal weight to every unknown, we get exasperated by the chaos. In either extreme, it's up to us to figure out the imponderables, or we're left with *blind hope*. Let's return to the Greeks and *Prometheus Bound* by Aeschylus:[5]

CHORUS: "Hast not more boldly in aught else transgressed?"

PROMETHEUS: "I took from man expectancy of death."

CHORUS: "What medicine found'st thou for this malady?"

PROMETHEUS: "I planted blind hope in the part of him."

Connection

Connection is centripetal—it draws in the other four principles and turns their attention to that which is most human and real. When we experience what others think and feel, and our leaders do as well, we have empathy. When our orientation is firmly rooted in reality, and our leaders are on the same page, we are grounded.

Deficient connection to other people excludes them, and they feel alienated. Excessive connection is the opposite, for we lose our privacy, our breathing room, and our individuality.

Reality is hard to pin down. When we can't pin it down, we choose not to make the effort, or we buy into a fantasy we would prefer take its place, we lose. Or when we make too much of what we know at the expense of admitting what we don't, we are oppressed, we replace facts with fear, and we're ground down.

Hope disconnected from people and reality is *foolish hope*. Leaders who are insensitive to conditions governing the real world and the interdependencies of others "are bound to hope badly and to act badly because of [their] hope."[6]

HOPEFUL DIAGNOSTIC PROCESSES

The process of self-assessment for hope must avoid the trap of starting from problems, pitfalls, and gaps. Rather than assigning blame, it's vital to appreciate what is hopeful in the situation. What does this mean in practice?

We can apply the principles of hope to understand where and to what degree hope resides. In doing so, we hold open possibilities as to what could happen if things were different and we are as inclusive as possible. Furthermore, we prefer working live and in real time, rather than assigning a process to a small group who might work behind closed doors. We will describe four ways leaders can perform hopeful diagnoses—all four are intended to practice hope's principles as they seek to help hope help.

Individual Soul-Searching

For times when you feel your hope waning, step back, get perspective, and lead from within. You can gather more information by asking yourself these five questions based on the five principles:

1. Is my vision really possible?
2. Do I have the ability to influence key stakeholders?
3. Is it worth the investment and sacrifice?
4. What's really true, and what might be unrealistic hope or wishful thinking?
5. Are there connections that I need to strengthen?

Small Group Dialogues

When you want to have a conversation around a table using the Golden Mean as a focal point, here is a three-step process:

1. Put up a Hope Scale from 0 to 10. Ask people to fill it in on three dimensions (you might provide them with three different color sticky dots):
   - Past (where we were 6–12 months ago)
   - Present (where we are now)
   - Future (where we will need to be in 6–12 months to achieve our goals)
2. Have a dialogue exploring peoples' interpretations, the meaning of the dots, how they explain the scale.
3. Now, use the Golden Mean and the five principles as a way to get specific about where there are opportunities to do things differently in order to catalyze hope.

Organizational Surveys

Organizational surveys can be analyzed, interpreted, and acted upon in ways that that are true to the five principles of hope. We've created an Organizational Action Survey to help gain focus. Here are three ways to use it:

1. Identify a group of associates who represent a "diagonal slice" of the organization including hierarchy, tenure, function, business unit, location, demographics, etc.,

and make the assignment to conduct interviews within the organization using the survey to collect data.

2. Name a group of promising middle managers and as a developmental project ask them to create focus groups to determine levels of hope in the organization. Ask for both qualitative information as well as quantitative data using the survey instrument.

3. Put the survey instrument on a website or use a survey vendor and collect information rapidly and broadly.

Organizational Action Survey

1. How much of a challenge are your work objectives?

SURE THING   1 — 2 — 3 — 4 — 5 — 6 — 7 — 8 — 9 — 10   IMPOSSIBLE

2. How many different ways do you have to meet your objectives?

JUST ONE   1 — 2 — 3 — 4 — 5 — 6 — 7 — 8 — 9 — 10   TOO MANY TO COUNT

3. To what degree do you feel engaged at work?

UNINVOLVED   1 — 2 — 3 — 4 — 5 — 6 — 7 — 8 — 9 — 10   FANATICAL

4. How many resources do you have to accomplish what's needed?

NOT ENOUGH   1 — 2 — 3 — 4 — 5 — 6 — 7 — 8 — 9 — 10   MORE THAN I NEED

5. How much does your job mean to you?

IT'S TRIVIAL   1 — 2 — 3 — 4 — 5 — 6 — 7 — 8 — 9 — 10   IT MEANS EVERYTHING

6. How important is the output of your work?

IT'S OF LITTLE VALUE   1 — 2 — 3 — 4 — 5 — 6 — 7 — 8 — 9 — 10   IT'S LIFE OR DEATH

7. How do you face unexpected events when they occur?

I BARELY NOTICE   1 — 2 — 3 — 4 — 5 — 6 — 7 — 8 — 9 — 10   I LOSE CONTROL

8. How do you handle problems that appear to be unsolvable?

I JUST DON'T CHANGE   1 — 2 — 3 — 4 — 5 — 6 — 7 — 8 — 9 — 10   I DO WHAT I'M TOLD

9. To what degree do you feel in touch with other people at work?

I'M EXCLUDED   1 — 2 — 3 — 4 — 5 — 6 — 7 — 8 — 9 — 10   I BARELY HAVE A LIFE OF MY OWN

10. To what degree do you feel things are being handled realistically?

IT'S A FANTASY-LAND   1 — 2 — 3 — 4 — 5 — 6 — 7 — 8 — 9 — 10   THINGS ARE MADE ALL TOO REAL

Appreciative Inquiry Processes

Appreciative Inquiry (AI) is an organizational practice completely in synch with the realization we came to back in the early 1990s that set us on our journey of hope: by paying too much attention to "driving out fear" we become fearful. By and large we find what we're looking for, even when we want it not to be there. AI says that "human systems grow toward what they persistently ask questions about."[7] We say, ask questions about hope!

AI is a cooperative search for what gives an organization life, and it involves asking questions in ways that uncover core strengths first and gaps only as byproducts. The point is to heighten a system's positive potential and build a platform for constructive change. AI has been used with thousands of people in large corporations with great effect as well as with small groups and start-ups. Designs need to be customized accordingly, but in all cases the heart of the process is the appreciative interview. It all starts when one person asks another a series of affirming questions. When these one-on-one interviews are repeated, and the answers accumulated, there emerges a groundswell of positive feeling, a web of interpersonal connections, and a trove of useful, positive information.

The questions we used in our interviews would work in any group, large or small, both to increase the power of hope. They presume an understanding of the five principles and an ability to make brief explanations.

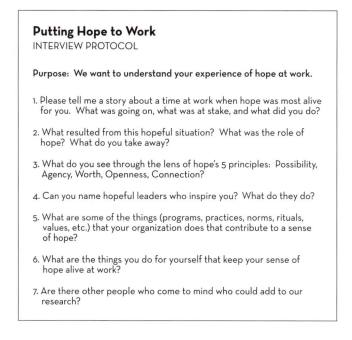

Putting Hope to Work
INTERVIEW PROTOCOL

Purpose: We want to understand your experience of hope at work.

1. Please tell me a story about a time at work when hope was most alive for you. What was going on, what was at stake, and what did you do?

2. What resulted from this hopeful situation? What was the role of hope? What do you take away?

3. What do you see through the lens of hope's 5 principles: Possibility, Agency, Worth, Openness, Connection?

4. Can you name hopeful leaders who inspire you? What do they do?

5. What are some of the things (programs, practices, norms, rituals, values, etc.) that your organization does that contribute to a sense of hope?

6. What are the things you do for yourself that keep your sense of hope alive at work?

7. Are there other people who come to mind who could add to our research?

In addition, we recommend the following Hope-Full Interview questions as a second method to accomplish the same purpose, without specific reference to the five principles. The principles are embedded in the questions rather than being highlighted.

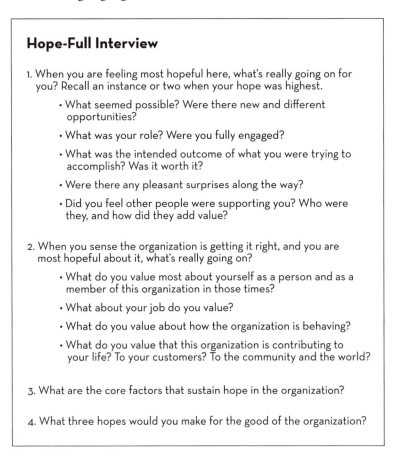

Hope-Full Interview

1. When you are feeling most hopeful here, what's really going on for you? Recall an instance or two when your hope was highest.

   - What seemed possible? Were there new and different opportunities?
   - What was your role? Were you fully engaged?
   - What was the intended outcome of what you were trying to accomplish? Was it worth it?
   - Were there any pleasant surprises along the way?
   - Did you feel other people were supporting you? Who were they, and how did they add value?

2. When you sense the organization is getting it right, and you are most hopeful about it, what's really going on?

   - What do you value most about yourself as a person and as a member of this organization in those times?
   - What about your job do you value?
   - What do you value about how the organization is behaving?
   - What do you value that this organization is contributing to your life? To your customers? To the community and the world?

3. What are the core factors that sustain hope in the organization?

4. What three hopes would you make for the good of the organization?

Section Three

Leading from Hope

Hope is an opportunity to be a player in the game.[1]

Stone Healer

Let's start with the results. Ten years ago, Haworth Inc., a $1.4 billion Holland (Michigan) based maker of office furniture, expanded into Asia Pacific. Haworth's investment was significant, including setting up the first wholly U.S.-owned manufacturing unit in China. Today, according to *Business Week*, "Haworth is selling locally all the office furniture it can produce in its Shanghai factory—even though Haworth products usually cost 30%–50% more than the models by local producers."[2] Sales in Asia Pacific have grown 50% annually for the past three years. According to Haworth Asia VP, Frank Rexach, "Business has started to explode."

The picture was not always so rosy. Four years ago, Haworth's Shanghai factory was operating at 20% capacity, struggling to gain a foothold in a rapidly commoditizing environment. Today, the company leads their competitors in Asia Pacific with the number-one brand selling to multinational companies who are setting up new offices, R&D campuses and factories in the high-growth markets of China, India, and other geographies in the region. What changed in the last four years?

The turnaround is attributed to a new, more unorthodox, customer-centric business model and marketing strategy. That explanation is necessary but not sufficient for understanding Haworth's Asia Pacific turnaround. There's a story beneath and around the business case: the leadership style and values of the person who implemented the changes. Frank Rexach exemplifies the qualities of a hopeful leader.

Frank, who grew up in a bicultural family, is a citizen of the world, having worked in North and South America, Europe, Asia, and Australia before moving to Shanghai in 2002 to head up Haworth Asia, Pacific. Fluent in

Mandarin, Frank was given the compliment of being called an "egg"—white on the outside but yellow on the inside. "That's my nickname in the factory. That's when I knew I was accepted."

For Frank, hope emanates from deeply held personal beliefs about the nature of relationship:

> "I view every interaction point with every human being as equally precious and valuable. They are all opportunities to listen and learn, to ask questions and to understand where someone else is coming from. All of us make up the body, not just the head."

These rich and abundant "interaction points" have both organizational and personal significance for Frank. As a leader, the cumulative learning he gets results in better decision making. Of greater significance to Frank is his belief that "magical things can happen" when those in positions of power or influence, "teachers, parents, managers," truly and authentically "use their role in life and work to affect positive change. Lives and hopes quickly become evident."

> "Caring is key. Everyone looks to develop from the inside out to move and progress in the world. For that to happen, each person needs to be nurtured, particularly given that we all come from personal and professional experiences where our self-esteem, this fundamental pillar in our being has been damaged from time to time.

> "Everyone comes to the task with some insecurity. We're all afraid to let others see what we don't know, but we all have gaps. As a leader you have so much positional power that has the potential to be abused, or not leveraged, or used hopefully to empower people and provide opportunities for learning, growth and increased self-esteem. All of us are looking for positive reinforcement of who we are as individuals. Everyone needs to have a voice."

To this end, before trying to change the business model, Frank ensured that his management team had the room to make their own decisions and develop themselves. Frank saw his role as "orchestra conductor," harnessing their energy. He "established the foundation first—built bonds of trust and feedback," before tackling business performance. Knowing his people would be on a steep learning curve, adjusting from a more hierarchical command and control model to one of distributed power, Frank showed his own vulnerability, staying present and open as a human being:

> "When I visit offices or the factory, I talk to people eye-to-eye as peers, 'How are things going' Even though they're not used to that

interaction culturally, it's still welcomed. I'm accessible, willing to share. I'll tell anybody anything. Transparency is key to building trust."

For Frank, taking this approach is as personally enriching as it is altruistic. He is energized and enlivened by "the mosaic of life—they give me hope and vice versa." Not surprisingly, this philosophy extends beyond the workplace to every aspect of Frank's life:

"If you connect with people, really connect, you learn so much. I have become so much richer because of the stimulative effect. It's all about what you, as a person, are willing to give."

Frank acknowledges that the kind of "unconditional caring and support" he strives to create in his environment is "counter-cultural in most companies—it's not just get me the numbers!" Currently, Frank's "EI" (Emotional Intelligence) is being assessed as part of a companywide program, but, he says, "I'm not sure you can measure someone's heart." Years of discovery have made Frank the person he is and strives to be, "a person of hope."

LEADERSHIP, CULTURE, AND HOPE

Frank lives and breathes hope's five principles. As a leader, he exemplifies many of the themes that emerged from our research. Who are hopeful leaders as people? What do they do to create a hopeful environment? How do they keep their own hope alive? To answer these questions, we made two assumptions.

Our first assumption is that anyone can be a leader. Clearly the higher you are in a hierarchy, the more influence you have by virtue of positional power. Or, as is more often the case with hope, it is most likely your immediate supervisor, the person you interact with on a frequent basis, who has the real power to open hope's door. Nevertheless, leadership is an activity independent of the pecking order.

The myth of organization culture presents it as a monolithic, inertial mass that exists outside of and separate from the people in it, and changes, if at all, with glacial speed. Nothing could be further from the truth. Yes, culture is embedded in an organization's systems, processes, and structures. For example, a reward system that values collaboration over competition reinforces desired cultural attributes. That reward system is not the culture, however, it is only an artifact.

Culture is what people do. The culture of an organization is created and recreated daily in every human interaction, no matter how small or seemingly insignificant. We are constantly shaping the cultures we inhabit by the choices we make, the values and beliefs we bring to every situation. It is in this "daily-ness" that the seeds of hope reside: "Everyone can influence hope in big and small ways depending on their realm of influence."

Our second assumption is that personal referral is an adequate way to find hopeful leaders. We put the word out to our many colleagues and asked them to recommend leaders who they felt created a hopeful work environment. To this list we added people who from our own observations fit the bill. And in the process of exploring stories of hope at work, we elicited our respondents' views of leadership in those situations. What we learned—the themes and patterns—cuts across many dimensions of organization (level and size, for-profit and not-for-profit status, geography, and industry) and individuality (age, gender, rank, and role).

BEING, DOING, AND STAYING ALIVE

In the final four chapters we describe leadership qualities and behaviors that make a difference in putting hope to work. First we address who hopeful leaders *are*—what personal characteristics make deciding differences in their success? Then we ask what these leaders actually *do*—how do they behave and what means and methods do they employ on a daily basis? Next we explore how they keep their own hope *alive*—what works for them and what can they teach us all? In the final chapter, we return to the beginning of our exploration and review central themes along the way—how does hope matter to leaders and their organizations?

"Quick, Bartlett! Instill them with hope!"

Chapter 11

Who Hopeful Leaders Are

You've got to have the miles in your legs to win a bike race—hope isn't enough.
Michael Conforti

Four qualities necessary for the leader who leads from hope emerged from our interviews: optimism, authenticity, altruism, and perseverance. Each is an important piece of the hope puzzle, and greater power came from the interaction of all four in the "bike race" of experience. We will illustrate each with a leadership story and associated material from our interviews. Then we will fit them into a framework of understanding based on character strengths and virtues.

OPTIMISM: MARSHA'S STORY

The Pfaltzgraff Co. started in 1811 as a small, local pottery. The privately held company was nurtured by successive generations of family members, growing to become the leading casual dinnerware company in the country as well as a significant employer in its York, Pennsylvania community.

Pfaltzgraff's president, Marsha Everton, describes the tabletop industry today as "pretty ugly on the hope scale. All the major brands are in a world of hurt." Competitors are for sale and stock prices are in steep decline. So when Marsha became president her vision was to rescue Pfaltzgraff from "commodity hell" through innovation and significant restructuring. The "organization was feeling bashed." Her goal was to "reverse the momentum of drifting down." To do this, she needed to reach deep into her own optimism.

Marsha paid close attention to "who was on the bus" because "so much of what hope is about is having the right people on board. You need people who share the vision and values and who go from having a job to having a responsibility." A turnaround in perspective and morale meant "reversing the cycle of decline and negativism," and that required surrounding herself with people who believed. "I'm in charge of optimism." Marsha says, so "let's look at it this way."

Being "in charge of optimism" while leading a turnaround with limited resources tested Marsha's resilience and creativity. She used stories like Apollo 13 to inspire ingenuity in desperate straits. She drew on her own resilience: "The greatest gift from my parents—pick up the pieces, change direction, and stay flexible. I kept coming back to having a plan."

Marsha had to make tough decisions:

> "The most depressing thing I had to do was close factories. It was the passing of an era. It breaks your heart. These are people who have given years and years of service."

Going through the "dramatic downsizing" of manufacturing, Marsha experienced the "downside of hope": denial that led to incrementalism.

> "We spent a lot of money and energy trying to beat the odds and propping it up. We couldn't see what was happening to us because these were our neighbors, a community of people, and this was not an academic exercise. Every job elimination was a headline in the local newspaper."

Through it all, Marsha's hope kept her focused on the long-term survival of a brand that has endured for 200 years:

> "The true worth of this company is its relationship with its customers— the emotional content of our brand. That connection is the heart of our product. I get all excited when I think like a customer. That's what keeps our people and me inspired."

In the end, the current leadership had to face the reality of lack of interest and involvement of the next generation of family members as well as poor financial performance. A difficult decision was made to sell the company.

> "As the President and CEO, I adopted the personal, hopeful perspective that this was a good decision for many reasons. This sale offered the opportunity to become part of a larger organization that could more effectively nurture the brand and the customer relationships and better deal with the turmoil in the total tabletop industry.

> "I believed and hoped that we could find a positive outcome for our employees, our customers and our brand. We focused our sale efforts on the brand story, our strong customer loyalty and the multi-channel

retailing capability that we had developed. We never stopped hoping and believing that we could continue the business, just with new owners. That hope required five months of working every day, every evening and every weekend, but we were successful.

"The Pfaltzgraff Co. was acquired by Lifetime Brands on terms that allowed the company to remain headquartered in York, Pennsylvania, and to retain the majority of our salaried staff. They even asked me to join Lifetime Brands and continue as President of a new Pfaltzgraff company that has responsibility for the multi-channel retailing of all Lifetime Brands products—an unexpected turn of events.

"I actually never hoped or believed that my personal position would remain after the sale. We put a lot of smart, hard work into our hope. We were fortunate to find a future that is now filled with hope for new business success as part of an innovative, growth-oriented, financially successful company."

Marsha and her staff, put a lot of "smart, hard, work" into their hope, but without Marsha's personal, unwavering optimism as a beacon, it's difficult to imagine people committing to an uncertain future. Getting to the other side of this situation required engaging the hands, hearts, and minds of her organization, which she elicited through her own passionate and positive energy.

> *Grant me the courage not to give up, even though I think it's hopeless.*
>
> *Admiral Chester W. Nimitz*

As another of our respondents said, "With hope, you're talking leadership." Seeing the big picture and seeing the positive side of it keeps leaders positive too." And another leader told us, "By temperament and disposition I'm a hopeful person, and that appeals to the hope in others." In the end, in the words of a third respondent, so much depends on:

"The capacity of leadership to remain hopeful and convey hope. I have seen organizations shut their doors when leadership doesn't have this capacity. Or meetings that run away with fear when there is inadequate leadership to regulate it with hope."

Always essential, the leader's own optimism as in Marsha's case is crucial in times when hope and fear hang in the balance.

AUTHENTICITY: CATHY'S STORY

Cathy Pagliaro is an Associate Director in Product Development for Procter and Gamble. Cathy has a breadth of responsibility spanning several consumer products categories, dealing with diverse cultures across the globe. For Cathy, the ability to be herself in her role and work culture is of paramount importance: "The day I can't be who I am at work is the day I must look for another job."

> "I am who I am. It's about treating others as you'd want to be treated. People are people regardless of their level in the organization. Early in life I had an experience that turned my life around. I realized you've got to do what you want and be happy because you could be gone tomorrow."

For Cathy to experience hope at work, her personal values must be aligned with the organization's values:

> "The person I am fits really well with P&G's corporate values and where we're going as a company. I am clear on the value I bring to my work and organization, and that freedom allows me to contribute and have fun. Recently people started telling me I was a role model. I like to think I am just enjoying the journey as the person I am meant to be."

Cathy describes herself as an "optimistic pragmatist." "Those who know me well know I often say 'It's a good thing.'" When you speak with Cathy, what comes across is her balanced perspective on life and work, a down-to-earth groundedness and candor:

> "My priorities are in the right place. I know I can always get another job, but not another family." (Cathy is the mother of four young children and married to a great guy!)

Her philosophy of leadership rests on openness, transparency, directness, depersonalizing issues, and keeping her energy positive:

> "You have to get grounded and make decisions, but you also have to be transparent about your choices, be consistent, and avoid a victim mentality. I try to lead by example. If I have issues I try to deal with them quickly.

> "I once had an issue where I had to get involved to help a coworker. She was deflated by the direction her project had taken based on what was happening on the business. I reminded her, 'It's not about you. It has nothing to do with your capability. It's bigger than both of us.'

> "Things don't have to be taken personally. It's not about us but rather, the work we do and the multiple influences coming together at any given moment that can point us in a new direction. People can and

should help each other. That's why assumptions about hierarchy make me almost angry. It makes it easier for people to distrust my intentions based on level, versus being open to how I can help them with a different perspective."

In the part of the world she manages, Cathy comes at work with a learning orientation:

"I'm big on talking to each other and learning from each other—making those linkages. In true development work, there are no failures. There can be fabulous learning from everything you do. I believe I instill that spirit—it's all about trying. That's what I love about my work in Product Development: it's a big puzzle."

In Cathy's environment,

"[s]aying, 'I don't know' is OK. People have to feel confident and secure enough to tell you that they'll go find out and come back with an answer."

At the core of Cathy's authenticity and hope is her belief in "knowing how to marshal your energy."

"You have to make the choice to do the hard things so you don't waste energy or create negative energy. I'm all about not wasting time on stupid stuff—being angry takes the life out of you."

Cathy has a "personal rule" that helps keep the balance:

"If I talk about a person or situation more than two times to other people, I have to go to that person directly to share what is on my mind or try to resolve the situation. Clear it out so it doesn't take brain space so I can be free to move on. I don't want to play games."

Cathy believes "Hope makes all things possible." In her organization, her goal is to create a win-win environment where people can be authentic, free to learn and stretch limits, and where the connection that comes from understanding each other is more important than agreement.

In terms of hope, the hallmark of Cathy's leadership authenticity is a willingness to engage personally and "expose that side of myself." As another manager told us:

"I have a style of reaching out to others—openly discussing, looking at things from many angles. You don't always have to be buttoned up and you can't compartmentalize your life. You are who you are. You need to bring your whole self to work. We spend a lot of time there so we can't be living a façade."

Undeniably, being real in an organizational context can be risky business according to another leader:

"There are moments when I'm scared to death. So to share with people and give them the space to bring it on has to come from an authentic place. It's not about fun and games; it's about being honest, and it's tough to be honest."

Authenticity for self and others is one root of a tree with many branches that include respect for diversity and tolerance of nonconformity. One executive used these words:

"When an organization lacks diversity, it runs the risk of valuing conformity over innovation, which ultimately leads to the loss of hope and confidence. The cost of conformity is learning to play it safe and going along to get along."

Authentic leaders invite authenticity for others, "openness, allowing feelings to be expressed, and no cookie-cutter expectations," we were told. "Hope flourishes in a culture that encourages authenticity."

Long before the word "authentic" came to mean genuine, it carried the meaning of "authoritative," as in something that has the authority of its original creator. Hopeful leaders derive their authority from their authenticity and are often described by words such as real, trustworthy, and genuine. They are "what you see is what you get."

Leadership scholars Fred Luthans and Bruce Avolio write that a leader's source of authenticity comes from both "*owning* one's personal experiences (thoughts, emotions, or beliefs, 'the real me inside') and *acting* in accord with the true self (behaving and expressing what you really think and believe). They've created a profile of authentic leadership—"the type of leadership needed in contemporary times"—whose elements are these:

1. being guided by end-values centered on the strengths of their associates;
2. closing gaps between what they say and what they do;
3. staying aware of their vulnerabilities and presenting themselves as human;
4. modeling confidence, hope, optimism and resiliency;
5. emphasizing developing personal development in their work; and
6. making judgments under conditions of moral complexity.[1]

The leader's authenticity functions as an invitation for people to be themselves. At the heart of this invitation is deep respect for truth and diversity and confidence in the future.

ALTRUISM: RICK'S STORY

Rick Ford started iHigh, Inc. in the heady, dot-com days of 1999. The initial vision was to create the capability to connect every high school in America through a network of websites, using advertising space on the web-based platform to fund it. For a year and a half, they grew and prospered. Then everything changed.

"One day, we will look back and realize how challenging the business environment was from 2000 to 2005. In the 90's, the economy was burgeoning, money was thrown at ideas, and there was a flood of prosperity. Suddenly, the fire hose was turned off. It was instantaneous—we pulled back on everything. Just as we were about to come out of that spiral, 9/11 hit—hope for the future of the business was at its highest and then the lowest. This was a real knockout blow for everyone. Again, we regrouped. We knew we had to keep focused. We were stunned. Business stopped. Nobody knew what to do. Things started to come back again, and a year later we went to war.

"Business leaders have to keep their group focused. Hope has to come from inside the organization."

How did he keep hope alive, for the organization and himself?

"It was a very emotional process. You have to question what you're doing personally and professionally in a tough business environment. It changed my priorities of hope—family and people are more important to me now, and they help me replenish the reservoir.

"A leader cannot show loss of hope, but that's difficult when you're digging deep to find it. So, you have a running conversation with yourself. The hope you have comes from many places. I went back to core beliefs, people, things that make us who we are.

"It's not until you run into a situation like this over which you have no control that you step back and take stock. Remembering you've had success in the past keeps that little flame of hope alive. Everyone brings something to the organization. The leader has to bring that eternal flame of hope. My biggest contribution was to bring that flame back in here with the help of friends, long talks and a thorough reevaluation of what we were doing and why."

Rick describes the "long, dark nights":

> "Everything we believed was challenged; everything we took for
> granted was shaken. I felt responsible for the organization continuing.
> I had to keep the darkness away. It wasn't a nuclear winter, but it felt of
> that magnitude. We went back into our caves, tried to put one foot in
> front of the other. As managers, we were trying to keep the tribe mov-
> ing forward and fed."

For iHigh, although the retrenchment initially had a scarring effect,
ultimately it was transformative. By successfully keeping the flame of hope
alive, the company evolved; it is now blossoming on a "bigger, better and
more solid foundation." The process reminded Rick of his Army Ranger
survival training:

> "You never knew how much you could do or withstand until you were
> pushed to the limits of your ability to survive. You never know how far
> you can go without giving up."

The transformation of iHigh is still in progress, but perhaps the most
significant shift is one of mission, away from a purely marketing orientation
toward a greater emphasis on education. One of their new ventures, Future-
Lab, exposes high school students to the latest advances and career
opportunities in science, math and technology:

> "We wouldn't have done FutureLab five years ago. It's an opportunity
> to create something meaningful in a business sense with long-term
> value if we can spark even one student per school. It changes who
> we are—gives something back. The first year we made no money,
> but we saw an opportunity to have impact on a generation. We
> didn't think that way initially"

Rick and iHigh emerged from their long dark night of the soul with a
renewed sense of energy, purpose, and passion. Hope now, is deeply
connected to the principle of worth:

> "Business for the pure sake of making money leaves you wanting. The
> feeling of accomplishment outside the bottom line, that's what
> you carry away. Recently I got my annual Social Security recap letter.
> There on one page was my entire work life income from the time I
> was fifteen. What's left? What have you contributed? I think it's
> the human condition to fear a life of insignificance, to leave no
> footprint. We want to feel part of something, to know we made a
> difference."

Altruism, concern for the welfare of others and putting shared purpose and enterprise ahead of personal gain, is a core quality of Rick as well as of this entrepreneur:

> "Even in the midst of chaos, people can feel hope if the leaders can provide them with that ray of light about the future, if the leader can demonstrate concern for the people and the organization and show them that things will get better and things will be ok.

> "People lose hope when the leader is self-centered and demonstrates a lack of caring about them or the future of the organization, or when people perceive the leader as not having enough smarts to make things right and turn things around. So, when there is hope present at work, it comes from people having faith that the leader is acting with wisdom and love for the organization and its people."

The research team at Case Western Reserve reported: "Hope prospers to the extent people put themselves in service to others."[2] The leadership field has indeed recognized the merits of this principle. Here is Steven Covey recommending leaders make a resolution to "dedicate my talents and resources to noble purposes and to provide service to others."[3] Robert Greenleaf's hopeful work, more than any other, has influenced the language of leadership in the direction of altruistic principles—thanks to him, the "servant leader" is standard practice and not an oxymoron.[4] In *Good to Great*, Jim Collins provides a model of altruistic leadership based on empirical research. He describes "Level 5" leaders—the highest level in his formulation, in the following way:

> "Level 5 leaders channel their ego needs away from themselves and into the larger goal of building a great company. It's not that Level 5 leaders have no ego or self-interest. Indeed, they are incredibly ambitious—*but their ambition is first and foremost for the institution, not themselves.*"[5]

Hope arises in response to knowing that those who care for us also care deeply about us.

PERSEVERANCE: CHANTHA'S STORY

Stung Treng province is located in Northeast Cambodia, on the top of the Mekong River at the Laos border. With a population of 90,000, Stung Treng is isolated, remote, and poor. The difficulty of obtaining an education, makes breaking out of the cycle of subsistence living and poverty highly unlikely.

In this setting the Stung Treng Women's Development Center (SWDC) was established in January, 2001. Originally conceived as a hospice for the terminally ill, it soon became clear that the solution for fighting AIDS in Stung Treng was to prevent its spread among healthy but potentially vulnerable women. SWDC realized that by providing an alternative, sustainable income to women (thus preventing them from entering prostitution) and educating them on health issues, the spread of AIDS could be prevented. Thus, the focus shifted from caring for AIDS patients in their last stages of life, to preventing AIDS in healthy young people.

Today, SWDC has evolved into a beacon of hope: a training and development center aimed at empowering women through basic literacy, health, nutrition, and child care education. In addition to basic knowledge, the center also provides training and support for marketable skills such as sewing and silk weaving in order to improve the quality of life through income generation. SWDC also supports children's education through day care and preparation for pre- and primary school. Through access to education, SWDC hopes to break the cycle of illiteracy and poverty in the family.

SWDC's Director, Chantha Nguon, herself the mother of two young children, is very clear that the women who wish to join her center (many more than they can accept), do so "with trust and hope for a better life once they finish the training." Getting through the program requires enormous commitment and "great difficulty" on the part of the women. "To reach that goal, they have to get through a one-year literacy and health education course, while working at temporary, low income jobs such as selling vegetables, cleaning houses, or planting rice." We asked Chantha what hope looked and felt like in her organization:

> "Once they become SWDC trainees, learning to sew and weave, they have to follow strict regulations: working hours, hygiene and sanitation, keeping the center clean, and working as a team by helping each other, which they've never learned before. Besides that, they are trying very hard (working extra hours and on holidays) to learn a new skill which requires them to deal patiently with thousands of small, fragile threads. Their hope when the term is finished is that they can produce good quality products to get a good income averaging between $40 and $80/month."

> *Hope is like a road in the country; there was never a road, but when many people walk on it, the road comes into existence.*
>
> *Lin Yutang*

To put that in perspective, Cambodia currently ranks 131st of 174 countries in the United Nations Human Development Index in terms of wealth, with 36% of the Cambodian population below the national poverty line of the United States.

Chantha and her staff work closely with each other and their students, building hope through a sense of community and shared responsibility:

> "We work with them as a team, and we always show our attention to each of them individually. We join their daily work, give good guidance, help them to find solutions for their difficulties, and create a nice atmosphere and place to work. On the weekend, we might have a picnic or dancing party.

> "We also have to be strict and fair sometimes, encouraging them to take responsibility so they feel they are members of the organization, not just beneficiaries. We have regular meetings with them to remind them of their roles within the organization and to let them understand they are not only here only for their own benefit. The organization needs their collaboration and commitment to survive."

Hope fires hope as improvement ripples out from the women SWDC serves:

> "Today we are providing for them, but it's not only changing their lives through sustainable income and knowledge of health, it's also helping to improve the situation of their families."

Finally, we asked Chantha what she does to keep hope alive. Her answer:

> "Taking responsibility and keeping hope ourselves. We have learned through experience that good works give good results. We're always trying to improve the quality of our products, seeking new techniques, designs and markets. We work hard ourselves in order to be an example for the women, showing them that everyone in the world has to work very hard to have a better life. We also need to have high commitment to achieve our goals, which is not easy all the time."

The courage and perseverance of the women who attend SWDC mirrors that of their leaders. There is no easy answer, only the hope that with very hard work, personal sacrifice, and commitment, tomorrow will be brighter than today. "We treat these women, who need help from us, with sympathy," Chantha told us. "Once their lives are improved, it also means our happiness is improved."

Hopeful leaders are courageous—they resist the temptation to compromise hope and they persevere in the face of adversity. We are reminded of Thomas Jefferson's description of the explorer Meriwether Lewis, as a man of "undaunted courage, possessing a firmness and perseverance of purpose which nothing but impossibilities could divert from its direction, careful as a father of those committed to his charge, yet steady in the maintenance of order and discipline . . . ."[6] Jefferson coupled courage with perseverance. It is this capacity to endure that connects courage, hope, and action. Senator John McCain, former POW, has observed: "If you do the thing you think you cannot do, you'll feel your . . . hope, your dignity, and your courage grow stronger."[7] Just as patience helps hope to continue and to endure, so, in return, hope helps one to be patient, to resist, to struggle. There is a reciprocal influence. Courageous in its desire, serene in its courage, hope is a principle of action.[8]

CHARACTER STRENGTHS AND VIRTUES

Optimism, authenticity, altruism, and perseverance—four strengths of character—are foundational for hopeful leaders. These attributes, significant anecdotally in our research, correlate with groundbreaking research begun in 2000 by Christopher Peterson and Martin E.P. Seligman. Their goal is nothing less than to describe and measure good character.

Working from the perspective of positive psychology, which relies on empirical research to identify and bolster human strengths in pursuit of happiness and the good life, the team analyzed basic texts on character rooted in the world's religious and philosophical traditions as well as influential surveys and secondary sources. The result is the groundbreaking *Character Strengths and Virtues* which classifies twenty-four *character strengths*, defined as the psychological routes to six universal *virtues*, which are the core characteristics valued over the millennia by moral philosophers and religious thinkers.[9]

Classification of Character Strengths[10]

Wisdom and Knowledge—*cognitive strengths that entail the acquisition and use of knowledge*

1. *Creativity [originality, ingenuity]*
2. *Curiosity [interest, novelty-seeking, openness to experience]*
3. *Open-mindedness [judgment, critical thinking]*
4. *Love of learning*
5. *Perspective [wisdom]*

Courage—*emotional strengths that involve the exercise of will to accomplish goals in the face of opposition, external or internal*

6. *Bravery [valor]*
7. *Persistence [perseverance, industriousness]*
8. *Integrity [authenticity, honesty]*
9. *Vitality [zest, enthusiasm, vigor, energy]*

Humanity—interpersonal strengths that involve tending and befriending others

10. *Love*
11. *Kindness [generosity, nurturance, care, compassion, altruistic love, "nice-ness"]*
12. *Social intelligence [emotional intelligence, personal intelligence]*

Justice—civic strengths that underlie healthy community life

13. *Citizenship [social responsibility, loyalty, teamwork]*
14. *Fairness*
15. *Leadership*

Temperance—strengths that protect against excess

16. *Forgiveness and mercy*
17. *Humility/Modesty*
18. *Prudence*
19. *Self-regulation [self-control]*

Transcendence—strengths that forge connections to the larger universe and provide meaning

20. *Appreciation of beauty and excellence [awe, wonder, elevation]*
21. *Gratitude*
22. *Hope [optimism, future-mindedness, future orientation]*
23. *Humor [playfulness]*
24. *Spirituality [religiousness, faith, purpose]*

The twenty-four "signature strengths" have been published as the VIA and websites have been created for people to go online and assess their strengths (for free); research data are rapidly accumulating. More than half-a-million people have now taken the VIA, and correlational studies are revealing several things. One finding reported by Christopher Peterson that has broad implication for us is that hope is one of the five character strengths most associated with indicators of happiness. Another is that the strength of vitality and zest correlates highly with hope and serves to amplify it. And in a study where 298 college students were asked to describe a time when they acted courageously and then to rate their action on each of the VIA strengths, hope ranked above all the others (save persistence, which is categorized as a strength of courage).[11]

The four attributes we describe as being related to who hopeful leaders are have a logical consistency within the "signature strengths" framework.

Optimism is one of hope's "companions." Authenticity, a correlate of integrity and honesty, refers to taking responsibility for one's actions and feelings, a component of the principle we describe as agency. Altruism is part of kindness, which is helping others. Of note, kindness is the single most endorsed strength among all twenty-four—perhaps it's the most human (thankfully) of all. And finally, perseverance means sticking to the task at hand over the long term, clearly an advantage when hope is at work.

This new orientation toward virtues and strengths should not be underestimated. In a world where social science finds "bad is stronger than good," and psychology focuses on disorder and disease, credible and sustained research in the arenas of what it means to be positively human and what it takes to go from good to better, from healthy to healthier, and from strong to stronger, indicates that we may be at the start of a revolution.

Chapter 12

What Hopeful Leaders Do

Hope is an attitude in action[1]

James Kouzes and Barry Posner

Who hopeful leaders are and what they do constitute the warp and the weft of leadership, to borrow an analogy from weaving. Running vertically, the long yarns of the warp form the foundation of the fabric. Constantly under tension, they must be resilient and strong. Optimism, authenticity, altruism, and perseverance are the warp, the foundation, of the hopeful leader's being.

Running horizontally, the weft creates the design, changing according to the creative vision of the weaver. Day-to-day leadership actions, the threads that bring hope to life, are the focus of this chapter. When we asked people to tell us specifically what hopeful leaders did that had such a beneficial effect, there was great consistency in the patterns they described. Generative actions that create growth and authentic connection are the fabric of hope, masterfully woven.

LISTENING, HEARING, AND RESPONDING

Jan works in the Research and Development function of a Fortune 100 company as a consumer insights specialist. She calls herself "a regular worker bee." Her story begins at the conclusion of a research project on women:

"I came away from it unsettled. What continued to stew in my gut was how little we did to affirm women's positive self-image."

A passionate advocate for customers, Jan bolstered her own research with secondary data, and "a collection of ideas flew together." Fired up, she requested time with Carole, a senior executive. Though Carole was many levels above her, Jan felt hopeful of getting a hearing, if only because they had worked together on a companywide diversity initiative.

> "I talked as fast and coherently as I could, presenting ideas about how we could treat women better and how we could communicate on a more personal level. I gave a couple of small product and packaging examples, all of which would strengthen the company's relationship with our customer.

> "Carole listened intently and interrupted often, saying things like, 'Of course! Why aren't we doing that already?' I felt deeply respected and validated. It made me very hopeful about the possibility of change in a big corporation—not only to improve our image, but to improve peoples' lives.

> "What Carole did next utterly surprised and delighted me. While I was in the room she picked up the phone and called two managers who headed divisions that made products for women to set up a meeting for the four of us, because 'Jan and I have been having a great conversation and I want her to share her ideas with us all together.'"

Carole coached Jan on writing a one-page executive summary of her ideas in preparation for the second meeting. The managers listened intently, so engaged that they extended the one-hour meeting by twenty minutes. The meeting was, for Jan, another "huge validation and moment of hope."

Within six weeks, everyone in Research and Development had been asked to rework their yearly objectives to reflect Jan's ideas:

> "They became the marching orders immediately. I felt tremendously appreciative that my ideas had legs. It made me hopeful that our customers would feel better about themselves using our products. I felt validated for having a brain that worked, and it made me hopeful that a large corporation could stop, take in new information, and make changes relatively quickly."

It's one thing to listen, another to hear, and still a third to demonstrate you have heard by taking action. Hopeful leaders listen both to the individual one-on-one and to the team by creating open, participative processes. In both cases, hope comes from the same source: "Feeling the leader wants my input and it's not an empty exercise." The person who is heard is validated; her contribution matters.

M. Scott Peck reminded us that attending to someone is an act of caring, and that "by far the most important way in which we can exercise our attention is by listening."[2] For the busy leader, and in a business world where time is money, the gift of attention is a demonstration of respect and caring. Benefits are reciprocal. Carole stayed open to new information and heard things that changed the game.

Ellen Langer, a writer, painter, and professor of psychology at Harvard, describes welcoming new information as one of the characteristics of a mindful state of being: "Behavior generated from mindful listening or watching, from an expanding, increasingly differentiated information base, is likely to be more effective."[3] It was St. Bernard of Clairvaux who said in the twelfth century, that if "you wish to see, listen; hearing is a step toward vision." Listening is the beginning. What really fires hope is when people see their ideas have impact, as did Jan.

At *The Cincinnati Enquirer*, publisher Margaret Buchanan works at building hope through collective processes. Open and participative, they embody both listening and being heard. One example is the mandatory employee survey. Before Margaret's tenure, results were never shared. She made it newsworthy by engaging a committee of employees to design it and develop a plan to make it useful. According to Margaret,

> "You have to give to get. Someone needs to listen; your opinions need to be valued. To keep hope alive we have to make sure the organization is addressing the needs of the employees, demonstrating commitment to them, and caring."

Inclusion is the hallmark of organizational processes that build hope. At the *Enquirer*, Margaret involved 100 managers in a three-year strategic planning process:

> "It was bottom up. They learned and were part of the planning so everyone bought in. We all emerged with a shared understanding of the context of decisions."

The president of Northern Kentucky University, Jim Votruba, used a similarly inclusive process to "get folks to dream about the possibilities." Called "Vision, Values and Voices," it was a strategic planning process involving hundreds of conversations inside and outside the university about how to shape the future of the community. Internally, Jim hoped all employees would "find their voice, to know they could make a difference in the organization. My biggest worry here is that fabulous ideas get generated in the ranks, and then shelved before they get to me."

Listening, hearing, responding—demonstrating inclusion, participation, openness, receptivity, and a willingness to change—make people feel hopeful. Journalist Brenda Ueland, a great listener, describes how it works:

> "When we are listened to, it creates us, makes us unfold and expand. Ideas actually begin to grow within us and come to life."[4]

Hope is the door opening, an authentic invitation to expand and grow. Hopeful leaders allow room for people to express themselves and engage in what is most vital to them. So it is that when hopeful doctors are asked by their patients "if there is any hope," they reply, "What is it you're hoping for?"[5] Perhaps the two most hopeful words a leader can offer are, "tell me."

PROVIDING CONTEXT

Context is our lens on experience. It shapes the meanings we make and the actions we take. Hopeful contexts empower, shedding light on possibilities and opportunities from the leader's vantage point. Particularly in situations where people cannot see the forest for the trees because they are too anxious, overwhelmed, or stuck, the alert leader can boost hope by reframing the context and adjusting the lens.

Randy Gier, an executive with Cadbury Schweppes, says,

"Creating vision is easy. The hard part is providing context, helping people see the positives. It's easy to see the negatives. Take for example, when your competition comes out with a new strategy. Don't switch to defense. Don't change the plan just because someone sent a panicked, 'Oh my God!' voicemail. You had a winning plan before. Stick with it. Consider your competitor's moves, but put them into context. They may be reacting to you! Have confidence in your own ideas and move on them first. Stay on offense. Don't wait for competitors to legitimize an idea that you can't get traction for internally."

Randy learned the skill of contextualizing from "the master," David Novak, former Chairman of YUM Restaurants. "What he taught me was when you put the customer first, validate peoples' concerns, and provide context for the organization, people will come along." Randy describes watching David work in a contentious meeting with franchisees:

"They had the votes. David listened first. He heard them out, and then stopped the conversation to help everyone step back. He started with the customer, reminded everyone of what we were trying to achieve, and then he went around the room person by person, validated what they had said and reframed their concerns in the context of serving the customer. He elevated the conversation to a bigger cause and got 100% alignment around our course of action."

Often, providing context and *reframing* shapes how you approach a problem, transforming an "Oh-my-God" moment into an opportunity. Todd

Tillemans, a general manager at Unilever, says,

> "We found out our major competitor made an acquisition that was game changing. By the end of the same day we had a very self-confident plan for how to take this as an opportunity. External challenges bring out the best. The things we uncovered in one day were comprehensive. We're playing to win."

Leaders who have been in the trenches can draw on their experience and longevity. They know nothing is as it appears initially; there's usually a buried opportunity. Sometimes, a turn of language reframes a negative into a positive:

> "We had a major new launch and it looked like we might not have samples ready. People said: 'There's not enough time. We *only* have ten days.' Instead of leaving them feeling helpless, I told them the good news was that we have ten *whole* days to figure out how to do it."

Sometimes, it's just reminding people how pieces connect to the overall vision. Keeping the big picture front and center reenergizes hope, according to this manager:

> "Most of us get pulled down into the day-to-day. What's going wrong now? We're not really hopeless; we're just stuck in neutral. We're wired to be detailed. We need to see how the daily connects to something bigger."

Another person said, "Having someone help us see the possibility at times when we can't see the forest for the trees sparks the imagination."

And sometimes providing context is mostly a matter of describing reality in plain terms, and being honest. Many of our respondents raised the specter of Enron: "It's devastating when a leader paints a picture and there's nothing behind it." Given the rise of cynicism and distrust in business, government, and the church, people are wary, which is bad news that could be good. There's good news if it means people are more discerning, bad if it means, as one of our respondents said, "People have battened up the hatches in organizations regarding hope."

When Anne Mulcahy became president of Xerox in 2000, the company was in big trouble, but she wanted to deal with the issues and tell the truth. She told analysts that the company's business model was unsustainable and that radical restructuring was necessary—Xerox's stock price promptly fell 60%. Then she met with employees and said, "This is going to be one of the most stressful situations of your life, so if your heart isn't in it, please don't stay." Xerox cut profit-sharing and reduced its workforce by 41%, but by the end of 2004 Xerox had halved its debt, moved into new, digital products, and created a cash flow of $1.5 billion—and Mulcahy is now chairman and CEO.[6]

Providing context helps people make meaning of a situation in ways that are more productive, inspiring, empowered, and hopeful. When a doctor lays out a diagnosis and a course of treatment for a patient, hope is enhanced and correspondingly the effectiveness of the treatment is increased.[7] Similarly, when a leader provides perspective, it builds a framework for action, a way to understand and gain perspective on experience.

Wilfred Drath and Charles Palus, researchers at the Center for Creative Leadership have written that leadership is meaning-making, a "process of making sense of what people are doing together so that people will understand and be committed."[8] Hopeful leaders invite people to look at situations in positive, opportunistic ways by providing context.

SAYING THREE LITTLE WORDS

No, not "I love you," but nearly as powerful in an organizational context when it comes to hope: "I don't know." People ask us what was most surprising in our research. The power of "I don't know" would have to go high on that list. Saying those three little words is excruciatingly hard to do in environments where people are expected to have all the answers and any sign of weakness is perceived to have consequences. Such a small thing, but so loaded with meaning, so hard to do, and so important to hope, as we were told:

> "I encourage my reports to say I don't know. I believe it for myself, but it's harder when I get into a meeting with my boss even though he says it's OK not to know. He means it, but it's very hard for people to say it. There's that underlying feeling that we should know."

One of our respondents told us of a manager she had who "introduced the notion of 'I don't know, but I'll get back to you.' People weren't bringing her the truth." The obvious downside of admitting you don't know is that it exposes you and makes you vulnerable. It's a risk. The gift of "I don't know," is the gift of truth, and where there's truth, there's hope. Here's a manager explaining:

> "Everyone comes to the task with insecurities. We're all afraid to let others see what we don't know, but we all have gaps."

The ability to speak the truth of one's experience is an invitation to authenticity. Being able to say, "I don't know," is the beginning of learning.

CHAMPIONING LEARNING

Peter Erickson is Vice President for Innovation, Technology, and Quality at General Mills, Inc. He "bakes" (pun intended) hope into the culture and processes of the organization he leads. Peter starts from the premise that "humankind is positively inclined, that individuals want to believe in the optimism of life, and they want to embrace the hope of a better future." His own style "taps into emotion," which he believes "is a far better tool than telling people what to do."

For Peter, innovation and change are the core work of Research and Development: "We're all about change; it's our lifeblood. If we don't change, we become irrelevant." Being on the leading edge of change requires a healthy dose of hope:

> "We must have a vision of the future that's hopeful, positive, engaging. It's especially critical when you're going through tough times. The innovation process is fraught with challenges. The vast majority of innovations don't succeed, so you have to create an atmosphere of hope and aggressive aspiration. I'd rather temper desire to try new ideas than have to stimulate it."

To create this hopeful and aspirational environment, Peter is "engaged by a learning philosophy" that permeates his organizational practices:

> "A lot of what we do is evaluate results. When I'm evaluating our results, I always ask, 'What did we learn?' regardless of what the results were. I don't want a mindset of risk aversion—playing not to fail instead of playing to win. Failures can ratify negative thinking: 'We shouldn't have done it' instead of creating a mindset of, 'Let's try again.' I see individual losses as an opportunity to learn and optimize our ideas for an even bigger gain."

Peter uses a variety of methods to nurture a learning culture. They are not elaborate, but they are mindful. Here are three of them:

Skip-Level Meetings

"Skip-level meetings" are meetings where a more senior person in the chain-of-command gets together with people who report at least two levels down—the direct reporting level is therefore skipped. The purpose is to encourage open and direct communication up and down the hierarchy by breaking lock-step expectations. Listen to the words of a Director in Peter's organization:

> "Peter called together 15–20 people one level down from his direct reports. He said, 'Here's the situation. The company is at a crossroads

and we need to do things differently.' He called a spade a spade and he was counting on us to help. That meeting was the essence of hope."

Peter is completely committed to openness:

"You can't inspire hope if you're viewed as someone not saying the truth. I talk about how we can win and what it will look like. To be a credible ambassador of hope you have to talk about realities, what is challenging us and what we must do to overcome our obstacles."

Stories

For Peter, stories are closely linked with the principle of possibility:

"Stories help people see through analogous situations that there is hope. We all love to hang onto examples. Storytelling brings it closer to home, closer to personal experience."

Two ways that Peter tell stories:

1. An annual calendar, "Food for Thought," is a holiday gift to his organization. Each of the twelve months tells a story from a peer in the organization, what they did and learned during their career and how it connects into a larger theme or example.
2. Personal Speaking Style: "Whenever I give a talk, I think about meaningful stories to tell. I believe that people often forget what you say, but they do not forget how you made them feel." Storytelling is a way to help people connect with an idea and feel something that becomes more lasting.

Communities of Practice

Peter brings together people with common areas of interest to have dialogue and learn from each other. These connections and networks, he believes, "accelerate hope." Peter believes it is the principle of worth that provides the link between the individual, the organization, and innovation:

"People want to leave something behind, a legacy, a mark. Incremental innovation isn't the kind of legacy that people leave behind. Even the most risk-averse want to be part of something bigger. It's a challenge in a public company where you're evaluated quarter-by-quarter, to balance the need to do things that are safe, incremental and short-term, with the opportunity for breakthroughs that are further out."

The connection between learning and hope is rooted in the universal desire to grow and develop. Our aspirations, our sense of self, our vulnerability all come into play when we are given the space to learn.

STORYTELLING

Peter's use of storytelling is a potent reminder that we learn best through analogies, "People love to hang onto examples." Sometimes, as in Peter's calendars, the stories are from within, close to home. Sometimes the inspiration comes from outside, as when Marsha used the story of Apollo 13 to show that incredible results can be achieved with few resources and an abundance of ingenuity. Sometimes, simply "having positive articulation within the company of good news stories, within the realm of bad news or numbers, spurs hope."

Stephen Denning, Director of Knowledge Management for the World Bank, is a great advocate of storytelling. Indeed, faced with the need to get a large organization enthused about major change, "Storytelling was the only thing that worked." Denning says stories have "round edges," making it easier for them to slide into our minds and lodge in our memory.[9]

Stories preserve the past of a community as well as its aspirations. Stories not only instruct by example, they are also vehicles for the transmission of values and guides to action. Hopeful, innovative communities are rich in "operationally enabling" stories, and hopeful leaders plant the seeds of the future as well as pride in the past whenever they have the chance.

ASSESSING PROGRESS

Hopeful leaders conduct what Jim Collins calls, "autopsies without blame."[10] In one large healthcare system that went on to win a coveted quality award, the CEO created a "blame-free zone where doctors and nurses could report their mistakes."[11] Judging was a crucial theme in the stories we heard:

> "There are different ways of coming to agreement on whether you achieved your goal—maybe something else came of it—you can take pride in other things."

> "Individual losses are an opportunity for bigger gain."

> "There can be fabulous learning from everything we do. I instill that spirit."

Although no less results oriented than other leaders, hopeful leaders demonstrate that process is as important as outcome. Ellen Langer writes that fixating only on outcomes can induce mindlessness. With more of a process orientation, "there are no failures, only ineffective solutions."[12] Validating the process of learning empowers people to continue stretching and taking risks, knowing that their efforts will not be categorized as either/or, success or failure. Assessment without blame builds confidence, capability, and hope.

CREATING SPACE

Hope thrives on elbowroom and is suffocated in environments characterized by:

"rigidity of attitudes, rules, overregulated, policies that don't give
credit for your brain. Rules are not necessary for most people. You
feel they don't trust you—you feel insignificant."

One space is expansive, door opening, innovative, while the other is con-
strictive, door closing, conforming:

"Unfortunately, just as children lose their creativity and willingness to
experiment as they grow older and are taught that conformity is "safer"
than standing out in the crowd, organizations lose HOPE when leaders
punish risk taking, innovation, and non-conformity."

All organizations have different kinds of work—some of it is about today,
some of it is for tomorrow. Some of it is well established, some is new. To a
great extent, the people we spoke with found hope in work that was new,
pioneering, and oriented toward discovery and growth. Many of the hopeful
stories we heard described
the opportunity to work in

How tight can life be without the space of hope?
Arabian Proverb

uncharted waters—an initiative, a project, or a phase of a
project that was exciting
because it was about finding
a way to do something better or bigger, unencumbered by the weight of
precedent:

"Hope is easier in a creative phase—everything is new."

"Doing something new—that's the easiest time to keep hope alive. You
have a spark of energy, and you're engaged in possibility. You're hope-
filled instead of being stuck in routine or feeling lost or complacent."

"Getting really focused on the customer and not being beholden to the
past—charting a new way—is what is engaging."

"There is a team of people involved in the hopeful endeavor, small
enough to create the special feeling of pioneering, but big enough
to overcome the loneliness of being on the leading edge of change."

"The ability to take risks in uncharted water is so refreshing."

"Having a blank canvas and tremendous latitude is hopeful. I can paint
a picture and have the freedom to execute against it."

These people are describing moments of freedom from constraints and from having to know it all. According to psychologist C. Rick Snyder, "learning through trial and error is a good means of raising hope."[13] Nowhere else in organizational life is trial and error as acceptable as it is when the work is new. Not everyone wants to be a pioneer, but for those who do, having leaders who are aware of spreading this work around and perhaps incorporating a bit of it into everyone's role, is a huge boost to the spirit.

HIRING AND PROMOTING THE "RIGHT" PEOPLE

"So much of what hope is about is the right people." Looked at from a different angle, one of our respondents said, "Eliminating a couple of people would really cause hope!" What we heard in our interviews was the importance of "handpicking a staff to create a hopeful organization. Hope starts at a high level and gets translated down." The people dimension of hope connects culture with authenticity: "Hope is nurtured when you see leaders acting in visible, obvious, genuine ways that are in keeping with our stated, desired culture." Hope rides in the balance when it comes to decisions of hiring and promotion: "Make sure they'll fit, authentically, genuinely." In terms of hope, "fit" is a function of values; when they are personally and organizationally aligned, both benefit. When they're out of sync, both lose. In organizations where symbolic significance is attached to who gets ahead or who gets which job, hopes rise and falls depending on the signals.

BEING PERSONALLY SUPPORTIVE

Leaders inspire hope by putting themselves—their time, their attention, their support—on the line. Kathi Seifert, recently retired as an executive vice president of Kimberly-Clark, summed it up: "You have to be out there, touching it—people have to see you really caring and carrying the load." Another respondent described her manager:

"He really backed me up, not only with money but with his time. He participated in every event. He walked the talk."

Contrast that with the experience of a third respondent who told us how deeply her own hope was affected by witnessing a colleague deal with an unsupportive manager. Her comments remind us how easily hopelessness, like hope, ripples outward:

"I have a colleague whose manager doesn't support her with senior management. He chooses to distance himself and misrepresent her work. The company loses more because she's a creative person who now won't venture out. This forces me to ask, why am I here? Why am I here late? My manager is not supportive. It's one thing to be facing a tough situation—rally, address the issue, meet the deadline. Then there's a lot of hope. But it's totally different if what's going on is completely uncalled for."

Sometimes, lending personal support is a positive, relatively easy gift. At other times it's more difficult, requiring a leader to take a stand. Listen to Andy Arken's story:

"In thirty-three years with one company, there were two situations that really stood out in my mind, where I took a controversial position and sent a recommendation to a high level. The first time, the executive looked at it and thought it was a piece of crap because I questioned what was being done in his organization. He emailed my manager saying I was irresponsible. I was dead meat. If you annoy a senior manager, you don't survive. My director told me I'd done the right thing and he'd take care of it (which he did).

"The second time, my manager got on the phone with me in the room and told the other person, 'Screw off. Andy's right and you're wrong.' He went to the wall for me, not without risk to himself. He did what he thought was right. I still get chills thinking of it. In the military you risk your life for your comrades. How rare it is in corporate America to take less serious risks."

Always be ready to make your defense to anyone who demands from you an accounting for the hope that is in you; yet do it with gentleness and reverence.
1 Peter 3:15–16.

Andy's managers had the courage to support him. That these examples stood out so clearly for Andy after thirty-three years in one company, is testimony to the hope-producing power of personal support. Another story comes from Susan Yashinsky's experience at Kmart. When headquarters was threatened with layoffs, Susan was fortunate to have a supportive manager:

"Every Monday morning he had a short meeting with everyone in his department, just to bring us up-to-date on what he could share. Mostly, however, these meetings served as a forum to alleviate the high anxiety among people not sure if they would be laid off. He told us that he had been laid off in his prior career and how you just go right to the bottom emotionally but then eventually rise up and find an even better job.

"It was a way for the group to share feelings, things we probably didn't want to express at home, and we all felt better after coming out of those meetings. It was what got us all through those stressful times. And, I believe it made us more productive for the company since we all went back to work feeling better and focused, instead of spending all day speculating on what might occur."

Here's the punch line of Susan's story: "Isn't it interesting that after thirty years of professional employment, this is one of the clearest and most profound events that sticks in my mind!" Even though he could not give people answers, Susan's manager could tell his personal story and offer support.

MONITORING HOPE

Monitoring hope is a constant diagnostic process on the part of the leader. More emotional and intuitive than rational, it requires mindfulness, paying attention to novel distinctions, signs, and cues. Karl Menninger described the process in terms that a leader can understand: "Diagnosing is the first step in a cooperative relation between patient, physician and environment ... based on hope, hope implicit in our effort and hope nurtured in our patient."[14]

Swedish researchers have found that hope plays an important role in our lives by helping us rebuild in the wake of tough times and pulling us through change: "Hope related to the life process has as its task reconstruction and transition."[15] Organizationally this means paying particular attention to monitoring hope as it relates to managing change. According to a respondent:

"This is a new language. One thing that's different is making hope more explicit. Thinking of it this way has caused me to be more aware of the emotional underpinnings of creating change."

Indeed, in the emotional underpinnings of creating change we look for hope to play a vital role in helping people bridge from today to the possibilities of tomorrow. William Bridges describes transition as the internal, mental, and emotional reorientation that accompanies external change: "Unless transition occurs, change will not work."[16] Transition begins with an ending, ends with a beginning, and in between there is the neutral zone, a limbo of sorts.

The propensity of organizations to regard reorganization as a panacea for whatever isn't working takes its toll on hope by keeping people in the neutral zone for prolonged periods of time:

"The constant reorganization, the uncertainty, not knowing, and not being focused, takes a toll. Your only hope is that maybe you'll have a job."

If uncertainty lingers too long, the sense that people have a modicum of control over their circumstances erodes. People tend to compartmentalize, according to Dr. Fred Loya, a psychologist whose practice includes many executives:

> "When you don't feel a lot of hope, you just worry about my world. You identify other things that motivate you. That's the rationale, how they talk to themselves, but the reality is, you can't just do that at work. You begin to do it in all parts of your life. You can't *not care* in just one place. If you turn off one aspect of your life, you go emotionally numb in all aspects of life. Once there's loss of hope it makes you vulnerable."

An example of sustaining hope through times of change comes from Sylvia Reynolds, now an executive vice president at Wells Fargo. Her story goes back to the early 1990s, when she was with another bank, but it's still fresh in her mind as a hopeful best practice. "It was one of the first big re-orgs (before 'downsizing' was a verb)." Over five years Sylvia had built a team that was well regarded, but the business was not doing well. "One day, a two-page memo came down saying we were superfluous. It could have been hopeless— that's how we felt at first, and scared."

Sylvia's creative response was ideally suited to the strengths of her people:

> "I asked the team to think about who they really were. They were a team of great marketers, so why not market ourselves? We created marketing campaigns to promote ourselves and our skills. The larger context was so painful—over 1000 people lost their jobs, which in 1990 was cataclysmic.

> "Because people were in touch with hope, they emerged galvanized, proud of their accomplishments, confident in their strong skills and hopeful of finding a job as good or better. One outplacement counselor called me after my managers arrived at the 'job hospital.' She said, 'We don't know what to do with your team. They're all in such good shape, we're not sure what value we can add.'"

Sylvia had created a positive subculture within the part of the world she could influence.

Another example comes from more recent times. It could be the back story of any number of newspaper headlines. This how one leader dealt with a potentially devastating blow to her group's self-esteem:

> "When our CEO was let go for wrongdoing, it was an assault on our personal integrity. It was very depressing, and morale was bad. We were ashamed to say we worked for the company. We had to get through that curve and realize we weren't alone and have the power to say 'That's not us.' We wanted our good reputation back. We empowered

ourselves to meet with our vendors and try to nip it in the bud. I'm a person with integrity, and it was important to accept what was happening and move on instead of letting things fester."

Not content to "let things fester," this manager took the bull by the horns. Faced with the choice of being victims or taking control of their world, she and her team chose hope. Sustaining hope through periods of dramatic transition and change is a necessity.

The good news is that hope does not arrive on a tablet from the mount. Hope is welcomed in a steady stream of interactions for which there are many opportunities every day. Hopeful leaders make the most of those opportunities.

Chapter 13

How Leaders Keep Their Hope Alive

I try to keep hope alive, but that's not always the easiest thing to do.[1]

Rosa Parks

Robyn Waters is known as the woman who helped "democratize design." Until she left in 2002 to write a book and start her own consulting firm, Robyn was vice president of Trend, Design, and Product Development for Target Stores, as described in *Fast Company Magazine*:

"She was the force behind the scenes, ensuring that Target's product mix was as current and fresh as the wares in retailing's tonier precincts. That was a startling innovation back in the early 1990's. Overseeing a large group of designers, she drove the look and feel that caught the media's attention and helped Target morph from a dowdy Midwestern discounter to the trendy 'Tar-zhay'."[2]

Robyn is, by nature, an agent of hope and possibility, inspiring people in organizations around the world just as she brought out the best in her designers at Target. But Robyn's hope, like all true hope, was hard won. She has seen the other side, and her journey to keep her own hope alive is testimony both to the human spirit and to the enormous toll any large corporation can exact on that spirit.

"I was a cheerleader of possibilities, at least of other people's if not my own. I worked very, very hard, and I was very successful. I worked so hard in fact that I stopped thinking about what I needed or what I wanted. I more or less disappeared, but not really. Internally, the stress and corporate politics were wreaking havoc with me.

"A friend pointed out to me that I was always filling other peoples' buckets, but what did I ever do for myself? Her point was that if you don't fill your OWN bucket, you have nothing left to fill others'. I had to learn the hard way that you can't 'give it all away' without replenishing yourself and still be vital. Basically, at Target I was running on empty. Nothing deadens the spirit or crushes hope more than that."

Robyn was losing herself:

"The cacophony in my head was so great, I couldn't find the real me anymore. I had gotten to a point where I cared more about what other people thought than about what I felt. I was so out of touch with myself. Like the proverbial frog that doesn't realize it's being scalded to death as you gradually turn up the heat, it all happened so gradually that I didn't see what was happening to me until it was almost too late.

"When I met others who still had their soul, I'd think, 'I want to be like that.' I sensed that they knew what mattered, what was important. I wondered what they have that I don't.

"Eventually, after a long process of evaluation and discovery, I realized that the life I was living was not aligned with my core values. I desperately wanted peace of mind, but I didn't know what that felt like or looked like."

And so Robyn embarked on a multidimensional program to find herself and her hope. She started yoga, which "did a lot to help me quiet my mind and become a better boss." She actively sought out different growth and learning models through what she calls "stories, heroes and demos." This included reading as well as conferences and events that "exposed my department and me to hopeful messages. I went for a broader perspective beyond the world of Target to bring some peace into my life and regain my soul." The stories helped her realize that she was not alone. "If they could do it, I could do it."

The "real turning point" for Robyn came in finding a coach:

"Who would not let me off the hook. When she heard 'corporate speak' as we worked together, she'd challenge me to find my *own* voice. She helped me figure out what was really important and helped me get back in touch with my long lost authenticity."

Robyn continued her journey motivated by her belief that to be a good boss she had to heal and rediscover who she was, by:

> "peeling away the curtain from the inside out. The silver lining here is that I became realigned with my values, which revitalized my hope, restored my energy, and opened up the floodgates of creativity. Today, I'm riding the crest."

THE BALANCED CONTAINER

How is it that hopeful leaders avoid becoming the proverbial boiled frog? Consider, at a visceral and spiritual level, the demanding work hopeful leaders do, and the enormous outflow of energy it takes. Certainly, as one of our respondents said, "You can't give energy without getting energy back," but there's an added dimension for those facilitating change in an environment of hope.

The leaders we speak of are, like Robyn, ambassadors of possibility. In that role, one invisible but critical function they perform we call, "holding the container." This means they create, sustain, and protect a space that can hold "transformative rather than destructive" human energy.[3] In that capacity, they must

- Cooperate with unfolding processes.
- Practice presence; stay connected.
- Stay present; keep returning to now.
- Slow things down as intensity builds.
- Embrace differences and dissent.
- Stay with discomfort.

Sometimes the container cooperates. At other times, anxiety and intensity build and the container wobbles mightily, calling for the leader's entire being to keep it centered and intact. This is not an easy job. It requires skill and patience, as the leader is always "running ahead" and finding ways to bring the organization along.

The hopeful leader, by definition a change agent, stands with one foot in today and one in tomorrow. "Standing in the tragic gap" is what educator Parker Palmer calls "holding the tension between the reality of the moment and the possibility that something better might emerge." Maintaining the stance requires stamina, personal belief, and courage, in Palmer's words. "I harbor no illusions about how hard it is to live in that gap. Though we may try to keep our grip on both reality and hope, sometimes the tension is too hard to hold."[4]

> *Perhaps the truth depends on a walk around a lake.*
>
>   *Wallace Stevens*

Maintaining a hopeful stance, particularly during those times when "you're digging hard to find it," requires constant attention to and care for one's own spirit. We heard this statement and others like it from many: "I have to constantly find hope for myself—fill up my bottle of hope." The key word is balance: "My strength is recognizing when positive and negative are getting out of balance." As soon as the scale starts tipping, this leader takes action to restore her equilibrium. A leader who is running on empty cannot be a catalyst for hope. When the pressure builds, and it becomes difficult to maintain the equilibrium of "standing in the gap," it's time to "Put on your oxygen mask before trying to assist those around you."

For us, the *second* rule of a change agent is to stay hopeful. (The first rule is to stay alive.) How do we increase our chances?

THE HOPE BUCKET

The beginning of replenishment is paying attention. As important as monitoring hope in the organization is remembering to take your own pulse. Here are words to that effect from a manager:

"If I don't have hope myself, I step back, get better perspective, perhaps realize I had false hope, or that my expectations were unrealistic. I reassess my objectives and that usually generates more hope."

Of course, taking your own pulse also means listening to yourself and trusting the information you're getting. The next step is having a rich assortment of options for your taking care of yourself. Here are some of the favorite ways our respondents refilled their hope bucket:

Consider Coaching

Coaches come in many forms. They can be supervisors, colleagues, mentors, old friends, life partners, or paid professionals. What's needed is someone with a trusted perspective who will tell you the truth. A coach should be there for you, with no agenda other than having your best interests at heart. Here are three different experiences:

"My coach tells me, 'I'm not here for the corporation—I'm here for you.' She's interested in my welfare, not in 'fixing' me for the company."

"I have consultants who are friends and trusted advisors. We talk a lot. They don't have their own agenda, or if they do, it's blatant and honest."

"Wonderful guides help me look at things with a slightly different lens and sense of proportion."

Good coaching can depend on sensing the right time to pose one of several "powerful questions"—open-ended questions that create the opportunity for discovery, clarity, a new framing, and ultimately action.

Powerful Coaching Questions

"What will success look like when you achieve it?"

"What's going well right now, and why?"

"How will you be thinking about this transition five years from now?"

"What resources are available to you that you've overlooked?"

"What possible ways are there to achieve what you want?"

"What are you most committed to?"

"What's the smallest thing you could do that would make the biggest gain?"

Build Networks and Sustain Relationships

Colleagues, family, friends—these are people who share a similar spirit. Isolation is the enemy of hope. Being on the edge of change can be "too lonely." These are the people you choose to surround yourself with.

How does Peter Erickson from General Mills keep his hope alive? Part of it is his optimistic nature and previous experience of "seeing things come true in other situations." But, the reality is "some days are darker than others." In those times Peter looks around him: "I am inspired by the quality of our people." He has a support system and uses it:

"I often lean on people who help me think through issues and together we find a way to succeed. We have a camaraderie that comes from being driven by a common spirit of growth and hope that helps with self-doubts. The community finds itself. The network is broad."

Another manager surrounds herself with people who "are not too conservative or negative—they drive me crazy." A third person reminds us of the importance of love:

> "I know hope is present when I can see even a tiny glimmer of light, a tiny possibility that there is escape from despair and a way to move forward beyond it. I've had a couple of despairing moments in my life when I just didn't think I had the energy to move forward. In both of those incidents it was the love of my daughter that pulled me through. What nurtured hope was my love for her, my responsibility to her, her love for me, and her need for me to be hopeful and happy. So, for me, love both nurtures hope and creates possibilities."

Reconnect Body and Mind

Health, wellness, rest, and humor are all components of being able to maintain a hopeful stance. Many of those we interviewed were forthcoming about their personal practices, for example:

> "I've found you really need to take care of yourself to maintain a clear-eyed view of possibility. When I'm healthier, not so exhausted, I'm more hopeful."

> "I started yoga to cope with the cacophony in my head. It did a lot to quiet my mind."

> "For me, to know hope is present, I have to quiet my mind. I listen to the "still" small voice."

> "Fear and limitations always enter when we are not listening to or trusting our inner guidance."

> "I take an hour a day to feed my creativity by working out my right brain. I can't do eight hours a day of left brain."

Medical research has shown that humor plays a role in healing. Being able to laugh is an important recovery mechanism. One of our respondents, with a notably wonderful sense of humor, said it was a lifesaver for her: "I take problems seriously, but not too seriously. It takes you out of the depths." Sometimes humor and delight can come at just the right moment and in just the right dosage:

> "The little joke, a positive email from a client, people surprising and delighting you with an insight or connection they make, a call late in the afternoon with good news—miraculous!"

Leadership researchers James Kouzes and Barry Posner write that one way credible leaders sustain hope is through laughter, finding "the comic in the tragic." Or it could be finding the sublime entangled with the ridiculous. Leaders know that "laughing—even when you are low—lifts the spirits."[5] We could all learn from Archbishop Desmond Tutu, one who knows how to savor the moment. His form of self-care is simple: he will dance, eat, laugh, and share stories when he gathers with friends—he "passionately embraces the gifts placed before him."[6] There are indeed many ways we can amuse ourselves, all for the sake of our health.

Focus on Others

Ram Dass and Paul Gorman's *How Can I Help?* is both a guide to service and a spiritual handbook to hope. How can we help? All we have to do is ask and then listen with an open heart. On one level, we help through what we do, but really we help by being who we are. "*We work on ourselves, then, in order to help others. And we help others as a vehicle for helping ourselves*"[7] (italics theirs). Three of our respondents would seem to understand how this works:

"Hope and help are intertwined."

"I focus on the young people who report to me—seeing them grow. I want them to do really well. I can make a difference to them by sharing things I've learned and helping them get recognized."

"In times when I can't find my own sense of hope, it helps to help someone else find theirs. I learn from watching their process of rejection and finally acceptance of possibility. Perhaps this is why so many religions and spiritual practices urge us to do 'good works'. The nurturing of hope and possibility in others teaches us how to help ourselves in all those ways. It's often easier to see someone else's potential than our own."

MercyCorp's Dan O'Neill says, "I keep my sense of hope alive through prayerful meditation early each day and through the intentionally practiced realization that reaching out to the less fortunate of our world is a transcendent, moral imperative that any of us can do to some degree."[8]

Hop with Hope

Nancy Kosciolek, a director at General Mills with twenty-four years of seniority, is by inclination and responsibility, often on the leading edge of change. The ride is a mental, emotional, and spiritual rollercoaster. Nancy's story reminds us that the best way for leaders to replenish their hope bucket is often near at hand.

"Threads, slivers of hope always come from people. Recently, I was feeling particularly empty and hopeless about work especially about what was required for innovation. Does anyone get it; get what it takes to really do things differently?

"I have learned to temper my frustration by looking for my next opportunity to catch a sliver of hope. As it turned out, I was having a four-hour meeting with a team I had been working with on developing a new product pipeline. My trust served me well. The team did a fabulous job at getting some rich information in their one-on-one interviews. The discussion among the team was deep and rich. We were all inspired by each other's stories. Humor played a key role in connecting us.

"Signs of hope were everywhere for the immediate project. And I was pulled out of my doldrums of 'they (the royal they) just don't get it.' It took the bits and pieces of individuals to spark my sense of hope on a larger level.

"Hope embodies the lily-pad approach to life. Hope. Hop. Hope. Hop. It requires boldness and courage. Just when your lily pad is getting swamped with water you need to spring out and hop to another pad. The pad is people. People. Pad. Jump in with people. Let hope come to you through your interaction with others. There is always, always a ray of hope somewhere within someone you interact with."

> *Faith, as I imagine it, is tensile and cool, and has no need of words. Hope, I know, is a fighter and a screamer.*
> *Mary Oliver*

Each of us has to find our own set of lily pads. Erik Erickson, psychologist of the human life cycle, reminds us that linguistically, hope *is* related to "hop."[9] From our first trusting steps we learn ways to persist and grow throughout life. The frog is back with us, now in playful form, hopping and hoping and not about to be boiled.

Conducted over five decades with a diverse group of participants, George Vaillant's longitudinal study of the basic elements of aging well has found that the factors that predict healthy aging are *lifestyle choices*, not factors such as ancestral longevity, parental characteristics, and body chemistry over which we have little control. What matters? No heavy smoking, no alcohol abuse, stable marriage, some exercise, not overweight, and "mature defenses":

"The first quality is future orientation, the ability to anticipate, to plan and to hope. The second quality is a capacity for gratitude and forgiveness, the capacity to see the glass of life half-full, not half empty . . . . The third quality is being able to imagine the world as it seems to the other person, the capacity to love and to hold the other empatheti-cally—but loosely. The fourth quality, related to the third, is the desire to do things *with* people, not to do things *to* people or ruminate that they do things to us."[10]

Each of us sustains hope in a uniquely personal way. The important thing is to find what works and practice it. Here are the words of a reflective manager:

"I have had to develop my own ability to support my path, no matter what happens on the outside. I think of the Serenity Prayer. We can only truly have control over our own actions and thoughts. When we learn to trust ourselves which may include a sense of trusting God or some spiritual essence, then we become so much freer to live the way we are called to live from deep within. This state breeds Hope like no other. And it also helps us to find hope and faith in outside situations that are unforgiving, scary, disappointing or even devastating."

The Serenity Prayer—to accept the things I cannot change, to have the courage to change the things I can, and to possess the wisdom to know the difference—is a prayer of discernment and moderation, hope's golden mean.

Chapter 14

Hope Matters

If there's a word I want to have registered here, it's hope.[1]
Brad Anderson, Vice Chairman
and CEO, Best Buy

We began work on this book more than ten years ago with a professional and personal curiosity about hope. How do hope, work, and leadership interact? When we asked managers about hope at work, the first response of many was: odd question. When we pursued it, stories emerged. We learned who hopeful leaders are, what they do, and how they sustain themselves. By listening to these stories and integrating research of past thinkers and present colleagues, we reached our conclusion, namely: hope matters at work, and leadership can be an act of hope.

We end with a focus on CEO-level leadership in the for-profit sector—a tough group of respondents. Remember the CEO in Chapter 1 who said:

"Hope has a negative connotation here—and so it's never been used. Hope brings ambiguity and conditions—we don't have room for that. It doesn't fit. Hope is not an emotion we want in the business."

Price Pritchett, a consultant and publisher of management handbooks, recently polled 312 for-profit and not-for-profit CEOs asking the degree to which "deep strengths" (including hope) are important to their organization's success. Although hope—defined by Pritchett as "faith in the future; favorable outlook regarding things to come"—was rated by the CEOs as an organizational strength, it was not considered to be very important as a factor for success.[2] Our view is that Pritchett's data jibes with the initial utterances of many of our respondents. Hope is not easily grasped.

Hope is nonetheless real. Some CEOs will go out of their way to use the "h" word, while others prefer to speak of hope's principles. We've shown how hope invites a remarkable range of expression. For CEOs, the issue is whether it can be a "force multiplier" to achieve results.

CUSTOMER CENTRISM

Best Buy is the Minnesota-based specialty retailer of consumer electronics—largest in North America, highly ranked in terms of growth, profit, and shareholder return, and highly ranked (second in its industry) on *Fortune* magazine's 2004 list of most-admired companies. Brad Anderson, Vice Chairman and CEO and 2005 winner of Gallup's award for positive psychology practice, speaks openly and intentionally about "unleashing the power of each individual person" and "giving people a sense of hope." We heard the words—what are the practices?

Best Buy attaches its success to the transition from "old school" to "new school," from selling products to customers to finding out what customers need. Good enough, but the real power resides in the people employed by Best Buy "unleashed" in their enthusiasm and creativity serving customers.

There are three steps in the Best Buy process, as Anderson described it. First create *space* for associates to learn about the business and even be educated in capitalism, and then endorse experimentation. Best Buy has measurement tools whereby each person in a store can create a customer hypothesis in a day and determine whether it improves sales or service. If things don't work as expected, that's OK. If they do, there are rewards. So for example, in one store a sales associate moved a hot-selling product to the front of the store and observed how the whole store benefited immediately. In another, an associate experimented with running ads in Vietnamese in the local community and discovered a new market. The "heart and soul" is to provide people an opportunity where they didn't have one by creating a safe place to deliver what they can.

Second, build on the *strengths* of each associate. Anderson admits it is hard to discover the individual gifts of everyone and to structure jobs accordingly. His two suggestions are to start where there is readiness either in stores or their managers to undertake this approach, and to be authentic no matter what. Their approach is realistic—start where you can and don't turn it into something artificial.

Third, tell *stories* about what is going on and communicate successes broadly. Best Buy has more than 100,000 associates, and as they expand around the world they use videos, leadership events, and informal word-of-mouth to communicate culture. So it's space, strengths, and stories, and according to Anderson, "If we can inspire people and provide a sense of hope, we'll have a powerful combination."[3] Our summation: *Hope provides a model for how to lead an organization successfully.*

LEGAL MATTERS

"Hope is a recognition that there are both bad possibilities and good possibilities—focusing on the good," according to Jay Zimmerman, chairman of Bingham McCutchen LLP, one of the twenty-five largest law firms in the United States and one of six law firms that made *Fortune* magazine's 2006 list of 100 Best Companies to Work For. The son of the president of the Famous Barr department store in St. Louis, Zimmerman leads the firm like the CEO of a major corporation.

One of the advantages of the corporate model is that it allows Bingham McCutchen to be decisive, and as a result the firm has grown quickly through acquisition. They're not "paralyzed by fear" when facing major decisions. They're the fastest growing law firm in the country—revenues tripled from 1999 to 2003 and then grew another 12% in 2004. "We analyze the downside first. If we have the tolerance to handle the worst case, we work at the upside." Zimmerman shows "constant optimism—a smile on your face can make a real difference."

"Hope comes in a variety of ways: partners who strive to be better than they are; associates who have a future; staff who are valued." Within the staff, they focus on success stories. "People know, people see."

We asked Zimmerman about hope's five principles, and these were his responses:

Possibility: "We have an aggressive, achievable goal: to be the best national firm in five to seven years."

Agency: "Everyone's a stakeholder, so we need to build consensus and buy-in."

Worth: "We have an obligation to over 2,000 families, and with the success of a business there is the opportunity to do pro bono work, make charitable contributions, and make this a better place to work."

Openness: "It's not all programmed—you've got to be good, and you've got to be lucky."

Connection: "A properly constructed workplace can be an enormously supportive system for people."

Zimmerman concluded: "Hope is at the confluence of the individual and the organization: a growing, optimistic organization with momentum, and individuals who are treated well and have access to opportunities." Our summation: *Hope provides effective principles for leadership.*

IRRATIONAL MARKETS

Jim Clifton, CEO of the Gallup Organization, is a major force behind the movement of positive psychology into the workplace. In his view, the new world of economics is split 30–70: 30% of the economy can be classified as a place where the old rules still apply—business in this space is driven by rational measures of productivity. But fully 70% of our world is "irrational" in the sense that traditional metrics don't yield enough information in order to compete at the highest levels. The top players in major market segments have financial data at their fingertips, but it's not enough for them to gain an edge—accounting, after all, is a trailing indicator.[4]

So, "soft" metrics are now more important than hard. When firms "max out on management innovation," the next frontier is related to how people *feel*. Building trust becomes a crucial competitive advantage because it increases organizational speed. Clifton sends an email to more than 1,000 employees each day, asking them to rank their positive energy level on a scale of one to five; it's a soft-measure way to ensure the hard survival of his firm.[5]

Seen in this light, hope's difficulty in being grasped—its "irrationality" as it were—becomes a competitive advantage. It is in the best interests of organizations in the "70% sector" to put hope to work. Not every organization will see it that way or be able to pull it off. Those willing to embrace the soft and squishy side of leadership—whether it is trust, hope, or some other "intangible" variable—may realize gains in their hard, independent variables: productivity, health and safety, and organic growth. Our summation: *Hope offers competitive advantage.*

FROM DILEMMA TO PARADOX

In Chapter 8, we described the paradoxical nature of openness and related recommendations from our respondents about how to "manage" a paradox—seemingly contradictory statements that may nonetheless be true. To learn more, we went to three CEOs and asked them to describe a paradox they see and live with daily:

> "Stephanie Streeter, Chairman, President and CEO of Banta Corporation: 'The more in charge I am, the less control I have.'"

> "Dean Scarborough, President and CEO of Avery Dennison: 'The more you standardize, the more freedom you create.'"

> "Geoff Martin, President and CEO of CCL Industries: 'The best business strategies ignore what competitors do.'"

Each of these paradoxes resists resolution, and in any case each of these CEOs would resist the attempt—complexity comes with the job.

Unlike a dilemma, a situation where the choices between options seem equally unfavorable or even mutually exclusive, the opposites in a paradox don't negate each other—they "cohere in serious unity at the heart of reality."[6] Effective leaders accept reality on its own terms, and they resist making gray things black and white. Rather than force a choice they search for a third way. They grant themselves enough slack to let things percolate when there is no obvious solution; they are comfortable enough in their skins to let contradictory thoughts and feelings coexist.

Here is an example of effective paradoxical thinking provided us by the leadership educator, Rob Hartz:

"The general manager of a trucking company wanted to purchase new global positioning technology that would help him keep track of his 220 trucks. The savings on fuel efficiency alone would be considerable. He was truly excited about the opportunity to have a better managed and more profitable company with the new equipment.

"He also felt a great deal of anxiety. Knowing how much the drivers enjoy their independence, he was concerned that the drivers would reject this approach. Experiencing the situation as a dilemma, he took no action.

"Over time, as he continued to reflect on the dilemma—the possibility of greater profit over against wasted investment and potential backlash from the drivers—he sorted out the full range of his feelings and thoughts, and he moved from dilemma to paradox. He realized that although he was focused on productivity, the drivers were motivated in other ways.

"Paradoxical thinking led him to a third way focused not on the new technology but on a new bonus program for drivers. By sharing financial gains with the drivers, he would make them partners. Now the technology would be a means to a valued end—the scorekeeper to help the company pay out bonuses."

"Paradox opens doors," according to Hartz, "it provides hope when things are stuck."

Hope is a bet on finding meaningful connections beneath seeming contradictions and it encourages leaders to consider complexity as an ally. How else do we explain it that people can simultaneously say "there is no hope," and "one can always hope"?[7] A seminal qualitative study on hope concluded that "hope and hopelessness are not opposite ends of one continuum nor is hopelessness the absence of hope . . . . Some sphere or dimension of hope is always present."[8] Although it may not be so obvious at first, hoping is coincident with "strong leadership" *because* it points toward paradox and calls up creativity. Our summation: *Hope offers innovative solutions to tough problems.*

MAKING HOPE HAPPEN (NOT)

The caution of CEOs to speak openly of hope may in fact be wise. Readiness is an important factor to consider before putting hope to work on a broad scale or even speaking of it first in the boardroom. Tom Yeomans, our teacher for years, has taught us: "Hope is the capacity to see the whole situation with a clear eye—the whole spectrum from bad to good—and stay connected." When hope is used simplistically or sloppily, it disconnects. Organizational assessment against the five principles of hope is a tough test—one worth taking before making hope the centerpiece of a corporate strategy or communications campaign.

So how then how does a CEO—or any organizational leader—make hope happen? Where does she start? We take our lead from Meg Wheatley, a writer and consultant known for her influential work on leadership and the new science:

> "We become hopeful when somebody tells the truth. I don't know why this is, but I experience it often."[9]

In the therapeutic realm, after touching the truth of their experience, people will often say they feel hope and renewed energy—even though nothing outward has changed. From our experience working with leaders and their teams, we've observed the following three phenomena:

1. A little honest dialogue floods the room with hope.
2. The experience of hope emerges through confronting real situations.
3. When leaders let themselves be human, hope comes in.

Hope is just not something a leader can "make happen" in the usual ways. It can't be commanded, directed, orchestrated, or managed. But when what's in the way is removed, it appears spontaneously. Lowering hurdles to hope is how to (help) make it happen.

Paul Pearsall, a psychologist and cancer-survivor, has written a book on the joys of hopelessness as a contrarian exercise in consciousness-raising.[10] Pearsall's views are actually closer to the essence of the matter than they are provocative—telling people to be positive, to exert mind over matter, and to have hope just makes it worse. As the teacher, therapist, and social activist Kathe Weingarten told us, "Trying to make people feel hope is completely wrong—leave their feelings alone!"

Leaders "liberate" hope when they attend to organizational ignorance, cynicism, or defense—topics where they can make headway by embracing rather than denying people's experience. Accordingly, the leader does more than set an example—the leader catalyzes. "Hope springs eternal in the human breast."[11] When "the fountain of hope" is flowing in the leader, the leader energetically releases hope in others. Our summation: *Hope addresses organizational realities.*

HOLD THE SHIP

The connections among leadership, hope, and work transcend single organizations and extend across cultures. In Thomas Friedman's book, *The World is Flat*, required reading for corporate CEOs, a Chinese official is quoted as saying, "Where people have hope, you have a middle class."[12] The comment suggests hope has geo-economic and political implications. Where there is at the very least a middle-class state of mind, there is the greater likelihood of stability, safety, and social equity. Hope holds a positive future that enables collective enterprise at the level of team, organization, nation, or world.

As profound as hope's positive impact may be in a flattened world, however, there is another dimension that may be just as far reaching. Here is where hope's capacity to include fear and realistically counter the negative has its greatest value—as a defense against extremism of any sort. It's a truism if not a scientific truth that those with no hope are prone to despair and acts of criminal desperation. We are saying more than that. *Hope is by definition the avowed enemy of extremism.* The hope scale holds hope's principles to the highest standard: the golden mean. By comparison, it's relatively easy to make things dualistic, simplistic, and polarized. Aristotle once again reminds us that "it is no easy task to be good."

> "For in everything it is no easy task to find the middle, e.g. to find the middle of a circle is not for everyone but for him who knows; so too anyone can get angry—that is easy—or give or spend money; but to do this to the right person, to the right extent, at the right time, with the right motive, and in the right way, *that* is not for every one, nor is it easy; wherefore goodness is both rare and laudable and noble.[13]"

After this passage, Aristotle quotes an order given by Odysseus to his steersman:

> "Hold the ship out beyond that surf and spray."

Since hitting the mean is so hard, we must "take the least of the evils," the intermediate position, the one most human. Hope holds our ship for a better day. Our final summation: *Hope is an orientation to a positive future that engages our heads, hearts, and hands.*

Appendix 1

The Interview Protocol

Purpose: We want to understand your experience of hope at work.

1. Please tell me a story about a time at work when hope was most alive for you. What was going on, what was at stake, and what did you do?

2. What resulted from this hopeful situation? What was the role of hope? What do you take away?

3. What do you see through the lens of hope's five principles: Possibility, Agency, Worth, Openness, Connection?

4. Can you name hopeful leaders who inspire you? What do they do?

5. What are some of the things (programs, practices, norms, rituals, values, etc.) that your organization does that contribute to a sense of hope?

6. What are the things you do for yourself that keep your sense of hope alive at work?

7. Are there other people who come to mind who could add to our research?

Appendix 2

Organizational Action Survey

1. How possible are your work objectives to accomplish?
   1____2____3____4____5____6____7____8____9____10
   Sure Thing   No Chance

2. How many different ways do you have to meet your objectives?
   1____2____3____4____5____6____7____8____9____10
   Just One   No Limit

3. To what degree do you care about doing your job?
   1____2____3____4____5____6____7____8____9____10
   Apathetic   Fanatical

4. To what degree do you have the resources you need on your job?
   1____2____3____4____5____6____7____8____9____10
   Not Enough   Too Much

5. How much does your job mean to you?
   1____2____3____4____5____6____7____8____9____10
   Trivial   Everything

6. How much does your work itself motivate you?
   1____2____3____4____5____6____7____8____9____10
   Irrelevant   Totally

7. How do you face unexpected events when they occur?
   1____2____3____4____5____6____7____8____9____10
   Don't change   Give In

8. How do you handle problems that appear to be unsolvable?
   1____2____3____4____5____6____7____8____9____10
   Ignore them   Get stuck

9. To what degree do you feel in touch with other people at work?
   1_____2_____3_____4_____5_____6_____7_____8_____9_____10
   Isolated   Too Close

10. To what degree do you feel things are being handled realistically?
    1_____2_____3_____4_____5_____6_____7_____8_____9_____10
    Unreal Made   Too Real

Notes

INTRODUCTION

1. Bob Herbert, "Get it Together, Democrats," *The New York Times*, October 17, 2005.

2. W. Edwards Deming, *Out of the Crisis* (Cambridge, MA: Massachusetts Institute of Technology, Center for Advanced Engineering Study, 1982), pp. 60–61.

3. Barbara Perry and Harry Hutson, "In the Company of Hope," *Journal for Quality and Participation*, XIX, No. 3 (1996), 8–13.

4. Reynolds Price, "The Look of Hope," in Hope Photographs, ed. Alice Rose George and Lee Marks (New York: Thames and Hudson, 1998), p. 172.

5. Karl E. Weick, "Careers as Eccentric Predicates," presented at the Society of Experimental Social Psychology, Champaign-Urbana, Illinois, October 11–12, 1974.

6. Richard Layard, *Happiness: Lessons from a New Science* (New York: Penguin Press, 2005).

7. Gregg Easterbrook, *The Progress Paradox: How Life Gets Better While People Feel Worse* (New York: Random House, 2003), p. xvi.

8. By Campbell Robertson, *The New York Times*, June 27, 2005.

9. By Michael Janofsky, *The New York Times*, August 1, 2005.

10. By Nick Cafardo, *The Boston Globe*, April 23, 2005.

11. By Patricia Nelson Limerick, *The New York Times*, June 22, 2005.

12. *Star Tribune: Newspaper of the Twin Cities*, April 4, 2005.

13. By Robert Davis, *USA Today*, October 19, 2004.

14. By A.O. Scott, *The New York Times*, October 5, 2004.

15. *The Boston Globe*, March 22, 2005.

16. By Stephen P. Williams, *The New York Times*, October 16, 2005.

17. Bruce Einhorn, "Listen: The Sound of Hope," *Business Week*, November 14, 2005, pp. 68–71.

18. By Virgina Heffernan, *The Boston Globe*, January 1, 2006.

19. By Ralph Blumenthal, *The New York Times*, January 18, 2006.

20. Editorial, *The Boston Globe*, February 1, 2006.

21. Thomas Bulfinch, *Bullfinch's Mythology: The Age of Fable, The Age of Chivalry, Legends of Charlemagne* (New York: The Modern Library, n.d.), pp. 15–17.

22. Max De Pree, *Leading Without Power: Finding Hope in Serving Community* (San Francisco: Jossey-Bass, 1997), p. 150.

23. Jacklin Eliott and Ian Oliver, "The Discursive Properties of 'Hope': A Qualitative Analysis of Cancer Patients' Speech," *Qualitative Health Research*, XII, No. 2 (February, 2002), 173–193.

24. James D. Ludema, Timothy B. Wilmot, and Suresh Srivastva, "Organizational Hope: Reaffirming the Constructive Task of Social and Organizational Inquiry," *Human Relations*, L, No. 8 (August, 1997), 1022.

25. James D. Ludema, Timothy B. Wilmot, and Suresh Srivastva, "Organizational Hope: Reaffirming the Constructive Task of Social and Organizational Inquiry," *Human Relations*, L, No. 8 (August, 1997), 1021.

26. "Donald E. Brown's List of Human Universals," in *The Blank Slate: The Modern Denial of Human Nature*, ed. Steven Pinker (New York: Viking, 2002), pp. 435–439.

27. Peter Geach, *The Virtues: The Stanton Lectures, 1973–74* (Cambridge, England: Cambridge University Press, 1977).

28. Christopher Peterson and Martin E.P. Seligman, *Character Strengths and Virtues: A Handbook and Classification* (New York: Oxford University Press, 2004).

29. Clifford Geertz, *The Interpretation of Cultures* (New York: Basic Books, 1973), p. 6.

30. Lionel Tiger, "Hope," *Hope Photographs*, ed. Alice Rose George and Lee Marks (New York: Thames and Hudson, 1998), p. 175.

31. Jerome Groopman, *The Anatomy of Hope: How People Prevail in the Face of Illness* (New York: Random House, 2004), p. 179.

SECTION ONE: CHOOSING HOPE

1. Peter Koestenbaum, "Freedom," City of Carlsbad, California Official Site, March 19, 2003.

2. Karl Menninger, "The Academic Lecture: Hope," *The American Journal of Psychiatry*, No. 116 (December, 1959), 481, 491.

3. Erik H. Erikson, *Childhood and Society* (2nd ed., New York: W.W.Norton, 1964); and *Insight and Responsibility* (New York: W.W.Norton, 1964).

4. Jerome Frank, "The Role of Hope in Psychotherapy," *International Journal of Psychotherapy*, V, No. 5 (1968), 383–395.

5. Ezra Stotland, *The Psychology of Hope: An Integration of Experimental, Clinical, and Social Approaches* (San Francisco: Jossey-Bass, 1969).

6. Louis A. Gottschalk, "A Hope Scale Applicable to Verbal Samples," *Archives of General Psychiatry*, XXX (1974), 779–785.

7. C.R. Snyder, "Hope Theory: Rainbows in the Mind," *Psychological Inquiry*, XIII (2002), 249.

8. Diane McDermott and C.R. Snyder, *The Great Big Book of Hope* (Oakland, CA: New Harbinger Publications, 2000).

9. Karen Dufault and Benita C. Martocchio, "Hope: Its Spheres and Dimensions," *Nursing Clinics of North America*, XX, No. 2 (1985), 379–391.

10. Martin E.P. Seligman, *Learned Optimism* (New York: Alfred A. Knopf, 1991), p. 49.

11. Rosemarie Rizzo Parse, *Hope: An International Human Becoming Perspective* (Sudbury, MA: Jones and Bartlett Publishers, 1990).

12. Patricia Bruininks, email message to author, November 11, 2005.

13. Studs Terkel, *Hope Dies Last: Keeping Faith in Difficult Times* (New York: The New Press, 2003), p. xv.

14. Martin E.P. Seligman, "Positive Psychology," in *The Science of Optimism and Hope: Research Essays in Honor of Martin E. P. Seligman*, ed. Jane E. Gillham (Philadelphia: Templeton Foundation Press, 2000), pp. 416–418.

15. James D. Ludema, Timothy B. Wilmot, and Suresh Srivastva, "Organizational Hope: Reaffirming the Constructive Task of Social and Organizational Inquiry," *Human Relations*, L, No. 8 (1997), 1026.

16. Christopher Peterson and Martin E.P. Seligman, *Character Strengths and Virtues, A Handbook and Classification* (New York: Oxford University Press, 2004).

17. Christopher Peterson and Martin E.P. Seligman, *Character Strengths and Virtues, A Handbook and Classification* (New York: Oxford University Press, 2004), p. 577.

18. Jaklin Eliott, "What Have We Done with Hope? A Brief History" in *Interdisciplinary Perspectives on Hope*, ed. Jaklin A. Eliott (New York: Nova Science Publishers, 2005), pp. 3–45.

19. Erich Fromm, *The Revolution of Hope: Toward a Humanized Technology* (New York: Harper Colophon, 1968), pp. 17–18.

CHAPTER 1: THE SIGNS OF HOPE AT WORK

1. Octavio Paz, *The Labyrinth of Solitude, the Other Mexico, and Other Essays*, tran. Lysander Kemp, Yara Milos, and Rachel Phillips Belash (New York: The Grove Press, 1985), p. 28.

2. Edward T. Hall, *Beyond Culture* (New York: Anchor Books, 1989), p. 34.

3. Maurice Lamm, *The Power of Hope: The One Essential of Life and Love* (New York: Simon & Schuster, 1997), p. 15.

4. Maurice Lamm, *The Power of Hope: The One Essential of Life and Love* (New York: Simon & Schuster, 1997), p. 15.

5. Darrell Rigby, "Management Tools," Bain and Company website.

6. Charles Handy, *The Hungry Spirit: Purpose in the Modern World* (New York: Broadway Books: 1998), p. 150.

7. James D. Ludema, Timothy B. Wilmot, and Suresh Srivastva, "Organizational Hope: Reaffirming the Constructive Task of Social and Organizational Inquiry," *Human Relations*, L, No. 8 (August, 1997), 1041–1043.

8. Rosamund Stone Zander and Benjamin Zander, *The Art of Possibility: Transforming Professional and Personal Life* (New York: Penguin Books, 2002), p. 108.

9. J.R. Averill, G. Catlin, and K.K. Chon, *Rules of Hope* (New York: Springer-Verlag, 1990), pp. 51–70.

10. Samuel Taylor Coleridge, "Work without Hope."

11. Joseph J. Godfrey, *A Philosophy of Human Hope* (Boston: Matinus Nijhoff Publishers, 1987), p. 11.

12. Carol J. Farran, Kaye A. Herth, and Judith M. Popovich, *Hope and Hopelessness: Critical Clinical Constructs* (Thousand Oaks, CA: Sage, 1995), p. 6.

13. Marcial Losada and Emily Heaphy, "The Role of Positivity and Connectivity in the Performance of Business Teams: A Nonlinear Dynamics Model," *American Behavioral Scientist*, XXXVII, No. 6, February, 2004), 740–765.

14. Fred Luthans, "The Need for and Meaning of Positive Organizational Behavior," *Journal of Organizational Behavior*, XXIII (2002), 699–701.

CHAPTER 2: THE EXPERIENCE OF HOPE AT WORK

1. Karl Menninger, "The Academic Lecture: Hope," *The American Journal of Psychiatry*, No. 116 (December, 1959), 486.

2. Karl Menninger, "The Academic Lecture: Hope," *The American Journal of Psychiatry*, No. 116 (December, 1959), 486.

3. Gabriel Marcel, *The Philosophy of Existentialism*, transl. Manya Harar (New York: Citadel, 1966), p. 33.

4. Jerome D. Frank, "The Role of Hope in Psychotherapy," *International Journal of Psychiatry*, V (1968), 383.

5. Lionel Tiger, "Hope," in *Hope Photographs*, ed. Alice Rose George and Lee Marks (London: Thames and Hudson, 1998), p. 174.

6. Luc Bovens, "The Value of Hope," *Philosophy and Phenomenological Research*, LIX, No. 3 (September, 1999), 667–681.

7. Richard Layard, *Happiness: Lessons from a New Science* (New York: Penguin Press, 2005), p. 167.

8. Joseph L. Muyskens, "Religious Belief as Hope," *International Journal for Philosophy of Religion*, 5 (Winter, 1974), 246–253.

9. Jim Wallis, "Faith Works," *The Impossible Will Take a Little While: A Citizen's Guide to Hope in a Time of Fear*, ed. Paul Rogat Loeb (New York: Basic Books, 2004), p. 203.

10. Jerome Groopman, *The Anatomy of Hope: How People Prevail in the Face of Illness* (New York: Random House, 2004), p. xiv.

11. Personal interview, Durham, NC, April 17, 2005.

12. Harold H. Oliver, "Relational Metaphysics and the Human Future," in *The Sources of Hope*, ed. Ross Fitzgerald (Rushcutters Bay, Australia: Pergamon Press, 1979), p. 197.

13. Max DePree, *Leadership is an Art* (New York: Dell, 1989), p. 11.

14. Gabriel Marcel, *The Philosophy of Existentialism*, transl. Manya Harar (New York: Citadel, 1966), p. 33.

15. Eva G. Benzein, Britt-Inger Saveman, and Astrid Norberg, "The Meaning of Hope in Healthy, Nonreligious Swedes," *Western Journal of Nursing Research*, XXII, No. 3 (2000), 303–319.

16. Peter Koestenbaum, "Freedom," City of Carlsbad, California Official Site, March 19, 2003.

17. Robert N. Bellah, and others, *Habits of the Heart: Individualism and Commitment in American Life* (New York: Harper & Row, Perennial Library, 1986), p. 66.

18. Amy Wrzesniewski, "Finding Positive Meaning in Work," *Positive Organizational Scholarship: Foundations of a New Discipline*, ed. Kim S. Cameron, Jane E. Dutton, and Robert E. Quinn (San Francisco: Berrett-Koehler Publishers, 2003), pp. 296–308.

19. Michael G. Pratt and Blake E. Ashforth, "Fostering Meaningfulness in Working and at Work," *Positive Organizational Scholarship: Foundations of a New Discipline*, ed. Kim S. Cameron, Jane E. Dutton, and Robert E. Quinn (San Francisco: Berrett-Koehler Publishers, 2003), pp. 309–327.

20. William Lynch, *Images of Hope: Imagination as Healer of the Hopeless* (New York: The New American Library, 1965), p. 28.

21. Charles Handy, *The Age of Paradox* (Boston: Harvard Business School Press, 1995), p. 252.

22. Jerome Groopman, *The Anatomy of Hope: How People Prevail in the Face of Illness* (New York: Random House, 2004), p. 201.

23. Daniel Goleman, *Emotional Intelligence* (New York: Bantam Books, 1995), p. 87.

CHAPTER 3: HOPE'S REWARDS

1. Lionel Tiger, "Hope," in *Hope Photographs*, ed. Alice Rose George and Lee Marks (New York: Thames and Hudson, 1998), p. 177.

2. Martin E.P. Seligman, *Authentic Happiness: Using the New Positive Psychology to Realize Your Potential for Lasting Fulfillment* (New York: Free Press, 2002), p. xi.

3. Roy F. Baumeister, Ellen Bratslavsky, and Catrin Finkenauer, "Bad is Stronger than Good," *Review of General Psychology*, V, No. 4 (2001), 323–370.

4. Thomas A. Wright, "Positive Organizational Behavior: An Idea Whose Time Has Truly Come," *Journal of Organizational Behavior*, XXIV, (2003) 439.

5. Shane J. Lopez, C.R. Snyder, and Jennifer Teramoto Pedrotti, "Hope: Many Definitions, Many Measures," in *Positive Psychological Assessment: A Handbook of Models and Measures*, ed. Shane J. Lopez and C.R. Snyder (Washington, D.C.: American Psychological Association, 2003), pp. 91–107.

6. Jaklin Eliott, "What Have We Done With Hope: A Brief History," in *Interdisciplinary Perspectives on Hope*, ed. Jaklin E. Eliott (New York: Nova Science Publishers, 2005), p. 21.

7. C.R. Snyder, L. Irving, and J.R. Anderson, "Hope and Health: Measuring the Will and the Ways," in *Handbook of Social and Clinical Psychology: The Health Perspective*, ed. C.R. Snyder and D.R. Forsyth (Elmsford, NY: Pergamon Press, 1991), p. 287.

8. H.S. Shorey and C.R. Snyder, "Hope as a Common Process in Effective Leadership," Paper presented at the UNL Gallup Leadership Institute Summit, Lincoln Nebraska, June, 2004, p. 8.

9. C.R. Snyder, *The Psychology of Hope: You Can Get There from Here* (New York: The Free Press, 1994), pp. 16–26.

10. C.R. Snyder, and others, "The Roles of Hopeful Thinking in Preventing Problems and Enhancing Strengths," *Applied and Preventive Psychology*, IX (2000), 249–270; C.R. Snyder, "Hope Theory: Rainbows in the Mind," *Psychological Inquiry*, XIII (2002), 249–275.

11. C.R. Snyder, "Hope Theory: Rainbows in the Mind," *Psychological Inquiry*, XIII (2002), 268–269.

12. Abraham H. Maslow, *Toward a Psychology of Being* (2nd ed., Princeton: D.Van Nostrand, 1968), p. 155.

13. Jerome Groopman, *The Anatomy of Hope: How People Prevail in the Face of Illness* (New York: Random House, 2004), p. xvi.

14. Jerome Groopman, *The Anatomy of Hope: How People Prevail in the Face of Illness* (New York: Random House, 2004), p. 193.

15. William M. Buchholz, "The Medical Uses of Hope," *The Western Journal of Medicine*, CIIL, No. 1 (January, 1988), 69.

16. Fred Luthans and Bruce Avolio, "Authentic Leadership Development," *Positive Organizational Scholarship: Foundations of a New Discipline*, ed. Kim S. Cameron, Jane E. Dutton, and Robert E. Quinn (San Francisco: Berrett-Koehler, 2003), p. 253.

17. Fred Luthans and Carolyn M. Youssef, "Human, Social and Now Positive Psychological Capital Management: Investing in People for Competitive Advantage," *Organizational Dynamics*, XXXIII, No. 2 (2004), 153.

18. Suzanne J. Peterson and Fred Luthans, "The Positive Impact and Development of Hopeful Leaders," *Leadership & Organization Development Journal*, XXIV, No. 1 (2003), 26–31.

19. Bret L. Simmons and Debra L. Nelson, "Eustress at Work: The Relationship between Hope and Health in Hospital Nurses," *Health Care Management Review*, XXVI, No. 4 (2001), 7–18.

20. H.S. Shorey and C.R. Snyder, "Hope as a Common Process in Effective Leadership," Paper presented at the UNL Gallup Leadership Institute Summit, Lincoln Nebraska, June, 2004, pp. 16–17.

21. James D. Ludema, Timothy B. Wilmot, and Suresh Srivastva, "Organizational Hope: Reaffirming the Constructive Task of Social and Organizational Inquiry," *Human Relations*, L, No. 8 (August, 1997), 1045.

22. Kim S. Cameron, Jane E. Dutton, and Robert E. Quinn, "Foundations of Positive Organizational Scholarship," in *Positive Organizational Scholarship: Foundations of a New Discipline*, ed. Kim S. Cameron, Jane E. Dutton, and Robert E. Quinn (San Francisco: Berrett-Koehler, 2003), p. 4.

23. David L. Cooperrider and Leslie E. Sekerka, "Toward a Theory of Positive Organizational Change," in *Positive Organizational Scholarship: Foundations of a New Discipline*, ed. Kim S. Cameron, Jane E. Dutton, and Robert E. Quinn (San Francisco: Berrett-Koehler, 2003), p. 227.

24. Ian I. Mitroff and Elizabeth A. Denton, *A Spiritual Audit of Corporate America: A Hard Look at Spirituality, Religion, and Values in the Workplace* (San Francisco: Jossey-Bass Publishers, 1999), p. 9.

25. Robert Galvin, "'A Deficiency of Will and Ambition': A Conversation with Donald Berwick," *Health Affairs: A Policy Journal of the Health Sphere* (January 12, 2005), Web Exclusive.

26. Virgil H. Adams III, and others, "Hope in the Workplace," in *Handbook of Workplace Spirituality and Organizational Performance*, ed. Robert A. Giacalone and Carole L. Jurkiewicz (New York: Sharpe, 2002), pp. 367–377.

27. "Human Resources: The Things They Do For Love," *Harvard Business Review*, (December 2004), 19.

CHAPTER 4: HOPE'S COMPANIONS AND COMPETITORS

1. Lance Morrow, *Evil: An Investigation* (New York: Basic Books, 2003), p. 266.

2. C.R. Snyder, and others, " 'False' Hope," *Journal of Clinical Psychology*, LVIII, No. 9 (2002), 1003–1022.

3. Sigmund Freud, "The Interpretation of Dreams," in *The Standard Edition of the Complete PsychologicalWorks of Sigmund Freud*, ed. James Strachey, and others (New York: Hogarth Press, 1954), Vol. V, p. 567.

4. Benedict Carey, "Can Prayers Heal? Critics Say Studies Go Past Science's Reach," *The New York Times*, October 10, 2004.

5. Sharon Jayson, "Power of a Super Attitude," *USA Today*, October 13, 2004.

6. "Spirituality and Health: Harold Koenig," *USA Today* live chat, June 29, 2005, 3:00 p.m. ET.

7. Benedict Carey, "Scientists Bridle At Lecture Plan for Dalai Lama," *The New York Times*, October 19, 2005.

8. Mark Hertsgaard, "The Green Dream," in *The Impossible Will Take a Little While: A Citizen's Guide to Hope in a Time of Fear*, ed. Paul Rogat Loeb (New York: Basic Books, 2004), p. 254.

9. Christopher Peterson, "The Future of Optimism," *American Psychologist*, LV, No. 1 (2000), 44–55.

10. Martin E.P. Seligman, "Positive Psychology," in *The Science of Optimism and Hope: Research Essays in Honor of Martin E.P. Seligman*, ed. Jane E. Gillham (Philadelphia: Templeton Foundation Press, 2000), p. 427.

11. Lisa G. Aspinwall and Susanne M. Brunhart, "What I Do Know Won't Hurt Me: Optimism, Attention to Negative Information, Coping and Health," in *The Science of Optimism and Hope: Research Essays in Honor of Martin E.P. Seligman*, ed. Jane E. Gillham (Philadelphia: Templeton Foundation Press, 2000), pp. 188–189.

12. Lauren B. Alloy, Lyn Y Abramson, and Alexandra M. Chiara, "On the Mechanisms by Which Optimism Promotes Positive Mental and Physical Health: A Commentary on Aspinwall and Brunhart," in *The Science of Optimism and Hope: Research Essays in Honor of Martin E.P. Seligman*, ed. Jane E. Gillham (Philadelphia: Templeton Foundation Press, 2000), p. 206.

13. Shelley E. Taylor and Jonathon D. Brown, "Illusion and Well-Being: A Social Psychological Perspective on Mental Health," *Psychological Bulletin*, CIII, No. 2 (1988), 204.

14. Cornel West, "Prisoners of Hope," in The *Impossible Will Take a Little While: A Citizen's Guide to Hope in a Time of Fear*, ed. Paul Rogat Loeb (New York: Basic Books, 2004), p. 296.

15. Fred Luthans and Susan M. Jensen, "Hope: A New Strength for Human Resource Development," *Human Resource Development Review*, I, No. 3 (September, 2002), 310.

16. Christopher M. Peterson and Martin E.P. Seligman, "Positive Organizational Studies: Lessons from Positive Psychology," *Positive Organizational Scholarship: Foundations of a New Discipline*, ed. Kim S. Cameron, Jane E. Dutton, and Robert E. Quinn (San Francisco: Berrett-Koehler, 2003), p. 27.

17. Julie K. Norem, *The Positive Power of Negative Thinking: Using Defensive Pessimism to Harness Anxiety and Perform at Your Peak* (New York: Basic Books, 2002).

18. John Braithwaite, "Emancipation and Hope," *The Annals of the American Academy of Political and Social Science*, DXCII (March, 2004), 84–85.

19. Benedict de Spinoza, "On the Origin and Nature of the Emotions," *The Ethics* (New York: Dover Publications, 1951), based on *Bruder's* 1843 *Latin Text*, Part III, Book 13, p. 1.

20. David Hume, *A Treatise of Human Nature*, reprinted from the Original Edition in three volumes and edited, with an analytical index by L.A. Selby-Bigge (Oxford: Clarendon Press, 1896), p. 439.

21. Francois duc de La Rochefoucauld, *Reflections; or sentences and Moral Maxims* (1665–1678), Wikiquote.org.

22. Alan Deutschman, "Change," *Fast Company* (May, 2005), 55.

23. Bill Breen, "The Six Myths of Creativity," *Fast Company* (December, 2004), 78.

24. Douglas S. Massey, "A Brief History of Human Society: The Origin and Role of Emotion in Social Life," *American Sociological Review*, LXVII (February, 2002), 25.

25. Stanley Rachman, "New Directions for Study" in *The Science of Optimism and Hope: Research Essays in Honor of Martin E.P. Seligman*, ed. Jane E. Gillham (Philadelphia: Templeton Foundation Press, 2000), p. 260.

26. Nadezhda Mandelstam, "Hoping Against Hope," in *The Impossible Will Take a Little While: A Citzen's Guide to Hope in a Time of Fear*, ed. Paul Rogat Loeb (New York: Basic Books, 2004), p. 342.

27. Quoted in Connie Zweig and Jeremiah Abrams, "Introduction: The Shadow Side of Everyday Life," *Meeting the Shadow: The Hidden Power of the Dark Side of Human Nature*, ed. Connie Zweig and Jeremiah Abrams (Los Angeles: Jeremy Tarcher, 1991), p. xix.

28. Dan O'Neill, email message to author, March 20, 2005.

29. Karl Menninger, "The Academic Lecture: Hope," *The American Journal of Psychiatry*, No. 116 (December, 1959), 490.

30. Lance Morrow, *Evil: An Investigation* (New York: Basic Books, 2003), p. 266.

31. Jeremiah Abrams and Connie Zweig, "Introduction" to Part Seven, in *Meeting the Shadow: The Hidden Power of the Dark Side of Human Nature*, ed. Jeremiah Abrams and Connie Zweig (Los Angeles: Jeremy P. Tarcher, 1991), p. 166.

SECTION TWO HOPE'S FIVE PRINCIPLES

1. Maurice Lamm, *The Power of Hope: The One Essential of Life and Love* (New York: Fireside, 1995), p. 22.

2. James R. Averill, George Catlin, and Kyum Koo Chon, *Rules of Hope* (New York: Springer-Verlag, 1990), p. 46.

CHAPTER 5: POSSIBILITY

1. Ronald Aronson, "Hope after Hope?" *Social Research*, LXVI, No. 2 (Summer, 1999), 489.

2. James R. Averill, George Catlin, and Kyum Koo Chon, *Rules of Hope* (New York: Springer-Verlag, 1990), p. 95.

3. C.R. Snyder, "Hope Theory: Rainbows of the Mind," *Psychological Inquiry*, XIII (2002), 251.

4. Marvin R. Weisbord, *Productive Workplaces: Organizing and Managing for Dignity, Meaning, and Community* (San Francisco: Jossey-Bass Publishers, 1987), p. 283.

5. Ian Fisher, "Old Foes, Pope and Dissident, Meet to Find Shared Ground," *The New York Times*, September 27, 2005.

6. Marvin R. Weisbord, "Applied Common Sense," in *Discovering Common Ground: How Future Search Conferences Bring People Together to Achieve Breakthrough Innovation, Empowerment, Shared Vision, and Collaborative Action* ed., Marvin R. Weisbord and 35 international coauthors (San Francisco: Berrett-Koehler Publishers, 1992), p. 7.

7. Claudia H. Deutsch, "If at First You Don't Succeed, Believe Harder: At Lunch with Rosabeth Moss Kanter," *The New York Times*, September 19, 2004.

8. Douglas Stone, Bruce Patton, and Sheila Heen, *Difficult Conversations: How to Discuss What Matters Most* (New York: Penguin Books, 1999), p. 115.

9. Barry Dym and Harry Hutson, *Leadership in Nonprofit Organizations* (Thousand Oaks, CA: Sage Publications, 2005), p. 149.

10. Robert H. Schaffer, *The Breakthrough Strategy: Using Short-Term Success to Build the High Performance Organization* (New York: Harper Business, 1988).

11. Jo Luck, telephone interview on February 2, 2005.

12. James R. Averill, George Catlin, and Kyum Koo Chon, *Rules of Hope* (New York: Springer-Verlag, 1990), p. 104.

13. Barry Schwartz, *The Paradox of Choice: Why More is Less* (New York: HarperCollins Publishers, 2004), p. 221.

14. Gareth Morgan, *Imaginization: The Art of Creative Management* (Newbury Park, CA: Sage Publications, 1993), n.p.

CHAPTER 6: AGENCY

1. Jerome Groopman, *The Anatomy of Hope: How People Prevail in the Face of Illness* (New York: Random House, 2004), p. 26.

2. Marvin R. Weisbord and Sandra Janoff, *Future Search: An Action Guide to Finding Common Ground in Organizations and Communities* (San Francisco: Berrett-Koehler Publishers, 1995).

3. Private telephone conversation on February 23, 2005.

4. Alex Kirui, "Jo Luck's Trip to Kenya," Heifer Project International internal memo, November 28, 2003.

CHAPTER 7: WORTH

1. Speech in New York, September 7, 1903.

2. James D. Ludema, Timothy B. Wilmot, and Suresh Srivastva, "Organizational Hope: Reaffirming the Constructive Task of Social and Organizational Inquiry," *Human Relations*, L, No. 8 (August, 1997), 1026.

3. Jean Baker Miller and Irene Pierce Stiver, *The Healing Connection: How Women Form Relationships in Therapy and in Life* (Boston: Beacon Press, 1997), p. 32.

4. Vaclav Havel, *Disturbing the Peace: A Conversation with Karel Hvizdala*, translated from the Czech and with an introduction by Paul Wilson (New York: Vintage Books, 1990), p. 181.

5. C.R. Snyder, and others, "'False' Hope," *Journal of Clinical Psychology*, LVIII, No. 9 (2002), 1013.

6. Thomas S. Bateman and Christine Porath, "Transcendent Behavior," in *Positive Organizational Scholarship: Foundations of a New Discipline*, ed. Kim S. Cameron, Jane E. Dutton, and Robert E. Quinn (San Francisco: Berrett-Koehler, 2003), p. 128.

7. James D. Ludema, Timothy B. Wilmot, and Suresh Srivastva, "Organizational Hope: Reaffirming the Constructive Task of Social and Organizational Inquiry," *Human Relations*, L, No. 8 (August, 1997), 1037.

8. John Hennessey, Susan Hockfield, and Shirley Tilghman, "Vantage Point: Look to Future of Women in Science and Engineering," *Stanford Report*, February 11, 2005.

9. Personal interview, La Jolla, California, March 1, 2005.

10. Charles Handy, *The Age of Paradox* (Boston: Harvard Business School Press, 1995), p. 159.

11. Charles Handy, *The Hungry Spirit: Purpose in the Modern World* (New York: Broadway Books, 1998), p. 71.

12. Barry Schwartz, "Pitfalls to a Positive Psychology," in *The Science of Optimism and Hope: Research Essays in Honor of Martin. E.P. Seligman*, ed. Jane E. Gillham (Philadelphia: Templeton Foundation Press, 2000), p. 410.

CHAPTER 8: OPENNESS

1. Jurgen Moltmann, *The Experiment Hope* (Philadelphia: Fortress Press, 1975), p. 20.

2. Ernst Bloch, *The Principle of Hope: Studies in Contemporary German Social Thought*, tran. Neville Plaice, Stephen Plaice, and Paul Knight (Cambridge, MA: MIT Press, 1986).

3. C.R. Snyder, and others, "The Roles of Hopeful Thinking in Preventing Problems and Enhancing Strengths," *Applied and Preventive Psychology*, IX (2000), 263.

4. Susan D. Bernstein, "Positive Organizational Scholarship: Meet the Movement, An Interview with Kim Cameron, Jane Dutton, and Robert Quinn," *Journal of Management Inquiry*, XII, No. 3 (September, 2003), 268.

5. Charles Handy, *The Age of Paradox* (Boston: Harvard Business School Press, 1995), p. 13.

6. Jim Collins, *Good to Great: Why Some Companies Make the Leap ... and Others Don't* (New York: HarperBusiness, 2001), pp. 83–87.

7. Jon R. Katzenbach, *Teams at the Top: Unleashing the Potential of Both Teams and Individual Leaders* (Cambridge, MA: Harvard Business School Press, 1998), p. 194.

CHAPTER 9: CONNECTION

1. Kathy Weingarten, "Witnessing, Wonder, and Hope," *Family Process*, XXXIX, No. 4 (2000), 402.

2. James D. Ludema, Timothy B. Wilmot, and Suresh Srivastva, "Organizational Hope: Reaffirming the Constructive Task of Social and Organizational Inquiry," *Human Relations*, L, No. 8 (August, 1997), 1026.

3. C.R. Snyder, and others, "The Roles of Hopeful Thinking in Preventing Problems and Enhancing Strengths," *Applied and Preventive Psychology*, IX (2000), 262.

4. Robert D. Putnam, *Bowling Alone: The Collapse and Revival of American Community* (New York: Simon & Schuster, 2000), p. 90.

5. Jeffrey K. Liker, *The Toyota Way: 14 Management Principles from the World's Greatest Manufacturer* (New York: McGraw-Hill, 2004), p. 37.

6. Stephen J. Spear, "The Health Factory," *The New York Times*, August 29, 2005.

7. E.M. Forster, *Howards End* (New York: Barnes and Noble Books, 1993), p. 157.

CHAPTER 10: THE GOLDEN MEAN

1. Comment made on teleconference in Authentic Happiness Coaching course, March 24, 2005.

2. Rick Klein, "Senate Moderates Forming Power Center: Deal on Nominees Could Spur Changes," *The Boston Globe*, May 23, 2005.

3. Aristotle, *The Nicomachean Ethics*, tran. F.H. Peters (London: Kegan Paul, Trench, Truebner, 1886), p. 55.

4. *The New York Times*, September 9, 2005.

5. Aeschylus, *Prometheus Bound*, The Internet Classics Archive.

6. Victoria McGeer, "The Art of Good Hope," *The Annals of the American Academy of Political and Social Science*, DXCII (March, 2004), 117.

7. David L. Cooperrider and Diana Whitney, *Appreciative Inquiry* (San Francisco: Berrrrett-Koehler Communications, 1999), p. 10.

SECTION THREE: LEADING FROM HOPE

1. Quoted in Lois S. Kelley, "Hope as Lived by Native Americans," in *Hope: An International Human Becoming Perspective*, ed. Rosemarie Rizzo Parse (Sudbury, MA: Jones and Bartlett Publishers, 1999), p. 256.

2. "The New Corporate Model," *Business Week* (August 22/29, 2005), 80.

CHAPTER 11: WHO HOPEFUL LEADERS ARE

1. Fred Luthans and Bruce Avolio, "Authentic Leadership Development," in *Positive Organizational Scholarship: Foundations of a New Discipline*, ed. Kim S. Cameron, Jane E. Dutton, and Robert E. Quinn (San Francisco: Berrett-Koehler, 2003), pp. 241–258.

2. James D. Ludema, Timothy B. Wilmot, and Suresh Srivastva, "Organizational Hope: Reaffirming the Constructive Task of Social and Organizational Inquiry," *Human Relations*, L, No. 8 (August, 1997), 1033.

3. Stephen R. Covey, *Principle-Centered Leadership* (New York: Simon and Schuster, 1992), p. 53.

4. Robert K. Greenleaf, *Servant Leadership: A Journey into the Nature of Legitimate Power and Greatness* (New York: Paulist Press, 1977).

5. Jim Collins, *Good to Great* (New York: Harper Business, 2001), p. 21.

6. Stephen E. Ambrose, *Undaunted Courage: Meriwether Lewis, Thomas Jefferson, and the Opening of the American West* (New York: Touchstone: 1997), p. 1.

7. John McCain, "In Search of Courage," *Fast Company* (September, 2004), 56.

8. S. Harent, quoted in Bernard P. Dauenhauer, "Hope and its Ramifications for Politics," *Man and World*, XVII (1984), 455.

9. Christopher Peterson and Martin E.P. Seligman, *Character Strengths and Virtues: A Handbook and Classification* (New York: Oxford University Press, 2004).

10. Christopher Peterson and Martin E.P. Seligman, *Character Strengths and Virtues: A Handbook and Classification* (New York: Oxford University Press, 2004), pp. 29–30; also www.authentichappiness.org VIA (Values in Action) Survey.

11. Cynthia L.S. Pury and Robin Kowalski, "Human Strengths, Courageous Actions, and General and Personal Courage," Poster Presented at the Fourth International Positive Psychology Summit, sponsored by the Gallup Organization, University of Toyota, and Toyota, Washington D.C., September. 29–October 2, 2005.

CHAPTER 12: WHAT HOPEFUL LEADERS DO

1. James M. Kouzes and Barry Z. Posner, *Credibility: How Leaders Gain and Lose it, Why People Demand It* (San Francisco: Jossey-Bass, 1993), p. 240.

2. M. Scott Peck, *The Road Less Traveled: A New Psychology of Love, Traditional Values and Spiritual Growth* (New York: A Touchstone Book, 1978), pp. 120–121.

3. Ellen J. Langer, *Mindfulness* (Reading, MA: Addison-Wesley, 1989), p. 67.

4. Brenda Ueland, "Tell Me More: On The Fine Art of Listening," *Utne Reader* (November/December 1992), 104.

5. Jacklin Eliott and Ian Oliver, "The Discursive Properties of 'Hope': A Qualitative Analysis of Cancer Patients' Speech," *Qualitative Health Research*, XII, No. 2 (February, 2002), 188.

6. Carol Hymowitz, "Should CEOs Tell Truth about Being in Trouble, or Is that Foolhardy?" *Wall Street Journal*, (February 15, 2005), B. p. 1.

7. Jerome D. Frank, "The Role of Hope in Psychotherapy," *International Journal of Psychiatry*, V (1968), 394.

8. Wilfred H. Drath and Charles Palus, *Making Common Sense: Leadership as Meaning-making in a Community of Practice* (Greensboro: Center for Creative Leadership: 1994), p. 4.

9. Stephen Denning, *The Springboard: How Storytelling Ignites Action in Knowledge-Era Organizations*, (Boston: Butterworth-Heinemann, 2001), p. xvi.

10. Jim Collins, *Good to Great: Why Some Companies Make the Leap ... and Others Don't* (New York: Harper Business, 2001), p. 88.

11. Parker J. Palmer, *A Hidden Wholeness: The Journey Toward an Undivided Life* (San Francisco: Jossey-Bass, 2004), p. 171.

12. Ellen J. Langer, *Mindfulness* (Reading: Addison-Wesley, 1989), p. 34.

13. C.R. Snyder and others, "False Hope," *Journal of Clinical Psychology*, LVIII, No. 9 (2002), 1016.

14. Karl Menninger, "The Academic Lecture: Hope," *The American Journal of Psychiatry*, No. 116 (December, 1959), 488.

15. Eva G. Benzein, Britt-Inger Saveman, and Astrid Norberg, "The Meaning of Hope in Healthy, Nonreligious Swedes," *Western Journal of Nursing Research*, XXII, No. 3 (2000), 312–314.

16. William Bridges, *Managing Transitions: Making the Most of Change* (Reading, MA: Addison-Wesley, 1991), p. 4.

CHAPTER 13: HOW LEADERS KEEP THEIR HOPE ALIVE

1. Ellis Cose, "A Legend's Soul Is Rested," *Newsweek* (November 7, 2005), 53.

2. Linda Tischler, "Masters of Design: Robyn Waters," *Fast Company Magazine*, No. 83, (June, 2004), 73.

3. Peter Senge, and others, *Presence: Human Purpose and the Field of the Future* (Cambridge, MA: SoL, 2004), p. 34.

4. Parker J. Palmer, *A Hidden Wholeness: The Journey Toward an Undivided Life* (San Francisco: Jossey-Bass, 2004), p. 175.

5. James M. Kouzes and Barry Z. Posner, *Credibility: How Leaders Gain and Lose it, Why People Demand It* (San Francisco: Jossey-Bass, 1993), p. 229.

6. Paul Rogat Loeb, "Introduction," in *The Impossible Will Take a Little While: A Citizen's Guide to Hope in a Time of Fear*, ed. Paul Rogat Loeb (New York: Basic Books, 2004), p. 10.

7. Ram Dass and Paul Gorman, *How Can I Help? Stories and Reflections on Service* (New York: Alfred A. Knopf, 1987), p. 227.

8. Dan O'Neill, email message to author, March 20, 2005.

9. Erik H. Erikson, *The Life Cycle Completed: A Review* (New York: W.W. Norton, 1985), p. 60.

10. George E. Vaillant, *Aging Well: Surprising Guideposts to a Happier Life from the Landmark Harvard Study of Adult Development* (Boston: Little, Brown and Company, 2002), pp. 305–306.

CHAPTER 14: HOPE MATTERS

1. Brad Anderson, "Managing a Strengths-Based Organization," Keynote Address, The Fourth International Positive Psychology Summit, sponsored by The Gallup Organization, University of Toyota, and Toyota, Washington, D.C., September 29, 2005.

2. "Deep Strengths Research Project," A Thought Paper from Pritchett, LP. 2005.

3. Brad Anderson, "Managing a Strengths-Based Organization," Keynote Address, The Fourth International Positive Psychology Summit, sponsored by The Gallup Organization, University of Toyota, and Toyota, Washington, D.C., September 29, 2005.

4. Jim Clifton, closing remarks, The Fourth International Positive Psychology Summit, sponsored by The Gallup Organization, University of Toyota, and Toyota, Washington, DC, September 29, 2005.

5. Ann Marsh, "The Art of Work," *Fast Company* (August, 2005), 78.

6. Parker Palmer, "There is a Season," in *The Impossible Will Take a Little While: A Citizen's Guide to Hope in a Time of Fear*, ed. Paul Rogat Loeb (New York: Basic Books, 2004), p. 120.

7. Jacklin Eliott and Ian Oliver, "The Discursive Properties of 'Hope': A Qualitative Analysis of Cancer Patients' Speech," *Qualitative Health Research*, XII, No. 2 (February 2002), 191.

8. Karen Dufault and Benita C. Martocchio, "Hope: Its Spheres and Dimensions," *Nursing Clinics of North Amercia*, XX, No.2 (1985), 389.

9. Margaret J. Wheatley, *Turning to One Another; Simple Conversations to Restore Hope to the Future* (San Francisco: Berrett-Koehler, 2002), p. 19.

10. Paul Pearsall, *The Last Self-Help Book You'll Ever Need: Repress Your Anger, Think Negatively, Be a Good Blamer, and Throttle Your Inner Child* (New York: Basic Books, 2005).

11. Alexander Pope, *An Essay on Man*, Epistle I, 1733.

12. Thomas L. Friedman, *The World is Flat: A Brief History of the Twenty-first Century* (New York: Farrar, Straus and Giroux, 2005), p. 375.

13. *Introduction to Aristotle*, ed. Richard McKeon (New York: The Modern Library, 1947), p. 346: *Nichomachean Ethics*, Bk II, Ch. 8, 1109a.

Index

About the Authors

HARRY HUTSON is a business advisor and executive coach, specializing in career development, change management, communication, and conflict resolution. He consults to a wide variety of corporations, nonprofits, and educational institutions. For over twenty years he was a leader in human resource management at Cummins, Avery Dennison, and Global Knowledge Network, and he is the Vice Chairman of the New England Center for Children. He has written articles on human resources and organizational development for a variety of business and professional publications and delivered numerous presentations and workshops to colleagues. He is coauthor of *Leadership in Nonprofit Organizations.*

BARBARA PERRY is a cultural anthropologist, management consultant, and teacher. In her twenty-five years of consulting to Fortune 500 companies, her emphasis has been on facilitating development of customer-focused, innovative cultures. She pioneered the use of team-based ethnographic methods both internally (for managing change) and externally (to develop customer-relevant product and marketing strategies). She is a frequent speaker at trend, market research, innovation, and product development conferences and also runs a leadership workshop for women. Her articles on organizational culture and learning, as well as on the use of team-based ethnographic research methods, have appeared in a variety of publications.